Finding
Herself

Ruthellen Josselson

Finding Herself

Pathways to Identity Development in Women

 Jossey-Bass Publishers

San Francisco • London • 1987

FINDING HERSELF
Pathways to Identity Development in Women
   by Ruthellen Josselson

Copyright © 1987 by: Jossey-Bass Inc., Publishers
                     433 California Street
                     San Francisco, California 94104
                             &
                     Jossey-Bass Limited
                     28 Banner Street
                     London EC1Y 8QE

Library of Congress Cataloging-in-Publication Data

Josselson, Ruthellen.
   Finding herself.

   (The Jossey-Bass social and behavioral science series)
   Bibliography: p.
   Includes index.
   1. Women—United States—Psychology—Longitudinal
studies. 2. Identity (Psychology)—United States—
—Longitudinal studies. I. Title. II. Series.
HQ1206.J67   1987   155.6′33   87-45414
ISBN 1-55542-049-4 (alk. paper)

Manufactured in the United States of America

Copyright acknowledgments appear on page 225.

JACKET DESIGN BY WILLI BAUM

FIRST EDITION

Code 8730

*The Jossey-Bass
Social and Behavioral Science Series*

Contents

Preface

When we consider women's lives, as I intend to here, no simple statements can be made. Beware anyone who makes them. My aim is to show the differences that exist among women, to show the aspects of their lives that must be accounted for in any adequate theory of female development.

Much of our knowledge of women is derived from the study of female psychotherapy patients and then generalized to all women. Not all women become patients, but patients come to represent womanhood. The nonclinical literature, some of it perceptive and wise, too often has its roots in the writer's personal observations of life or the experiences of friends and colleagues.

I have come to the conclusion that female psychologists, although somewhat more cognizant of female experience than male psychologists, are also not representative of all women. Those of us who choose to devote a significant portion of our existence to the understanding of psychological experience become different in important ways from those who do not. We probe deeply, look beneath apparent reality, question appearances, and are quick to label phenomena as being other than what they seem. Most of us tend to continuously examine ourselves, by inclination as well as by training. We wonder about the universal and theoretical implications of our most private experiences. No evidence indicates that we do any better at life than anyone else, but we are different. As we grow more deeply into our field, we increasingly surround ourselves with people

who think as we do. Eventually, we lose touch with other ways
of experiencing and thinking and become increasingly isolated
from those very people whom our theories purport to understand.

Psychology at present has no theory of normal development in women. We have statistical studies that examine how
one variable goes with another, and survey studies filled with
percentages rather than with people. We have life-history studies of patients. But we do not have the intensive data on normal
women on which any theory must be based. Most often, psychological writers who wish to consider phenomena among normal women turn to novels for characters to illustrate their
points. This book is intended to provide some of the data that
are needed, as a step toward the development of theory.

In this book, I consider identity development among a
representative sample of college-educated women. Although my
research design is grounded in Eriksonian and object-relations
theory, the interview format and data analysis leave open the
possibility of discovery. I wanted my subjects to tell me what
was most important to their sense of themselves, to their identity.

When a psychologist deals with normal individuals, with
nonpatients, the usual classification schemes are no longer useful. Psychology has few theoretical yardsticks with which to
measure and evaluate lives in progress. To write about normal
people living out their lives, we must use ordinary descriptive
words, and here biases are likely to creep in. Although I have
endeavored to remain as objective as possible in considering the
lives of these women, such objectivity is impossible to attain
fully. Therefore, it is best to state my biases at the outset.

Trained as both a clinical and a developmental psychologist
in the psychoanalytic tradition, I grafted humanistic and existential viewpoints onto my way of thinking about people. I believe
that the past shapes the present, largely through unconscious
forces. I also believe that people can disentangle themselves
from past conflicts with optimal environmental influences, including psychotherapy among many possibilities. I value
growth and self-actualization. I construct human personality

within a developmental framework that posits psychological tasks and internal change as the person grows. Therefore, I tend to view higher or more mature forms of psychological development as healthy and desirable, even though I recognize that many people live happy, productive lives at developmental levels that I would not judge to be advanced.

I wish I could talk about higher or lower levels of development without implying better or worse. My intention in this book is to describe phenomena and to try to understand what underlies them. As a psychologist, I do not know better than anyone else how life ought to be lived. If I seem to be saying that I do, please ignore it.

The Plan of This Book

Finding Herself is a longitudinal study of the development of identity in women. From 1971 to 1973, I conducted intensive interviews with sixty randomly selected senior women from four colleges and universities. At that time, I assessed each woman's progress in formulating identity as well as aspects of her developmental history. Twelve years later, I was able to locate and interview thirty-four of these women in an effort to understand how their adolescent identity formation influenced their lives. (Details of the methodology are provided in the Appendixes.) Both in interviewing and in data analysis, I applied the tools of clinical psychology to try to understand a nonpatient population.

Two interrelated themes underlie this work. The first represents an effort to extend our theoretical understanding of the developmentally crucial process of identity formation, to respond to Erik Erikson's statement that "in order to describe the universal genetics of identity, one would wish to be able to trace its development through the life histories of 'ordinary' individuals" (1968, p. 155). The "ordinary" individuals I have chosen to study are women, and this choice forms the second motif. Despite all that has been written about women, few have studied women phenomenologically or have been interested in their self-definition, allowing them to tell their stories. In this respect, this work is fundamentally heuristic, an effort to portray the whole woman who is lost in statistical analyses.

In the opening chapter, I explore some of the questions that plague our effort to develop an adequate psychology of women and argue that the holistic concept of identity encompasses the major issues with which women struggle from adolescence into adulthood.

The second chapter reviews the theoretical underpinnings by reconsidering the seminal contributions of Erikson and integrating these ideas with concepts from object-relations theory regarding separation and individuation. I review these theories specifically with respect to their applicability to an understanding of women.

For this study, I used an empirical research paradigm known as identity-status research, a paradigm that preserves the nuance and subtlety of Erikson's work. As discussed in Chapter Three, this approach identifies four divergent paths to identity formation, based on the presence or absence of crisis about and commitment to specific identity elements.

Most of this book is devoted to an exploration of the lives of women who follow each of the four paths. Detailed case material is presented in order to provide an intact view of a life in progress as well as to illustrate commonalities among the women within a group. In Chapter Four, I discuss women who have formulated identity without a period of crisis, who have carried forward childhood-based self-definitions and avoided the rethinking that adolescence usually requires. The longitudinal data provide some answer to the question of whether they experience crisis later on.

Chapter Five considers women who have traversed a period of identity crisis and successfully forged identity on their own terms. This chapter considers both the developmental strengths that presage identity resolution and the consequences of self-determined identity for adulthood. Some women remained in a state of identity crisis at the end of college; Chapter Six explores the resolutions that they eventually found. Women who had not made identity decisions by the end of college nor were struggling to make them, experiencing neither crisis nor commitment, are the subjects of Chapter Seven. These latter two groups are the ones most familiar to therapists.

In a concluding chapter, I reflect on the issues that have emerged as most crucial to identity in women. The women in this study, whom I came to know deeply, taught me much about what we, as developmental psychologists and therapists, must ponder in order to understand the psychology of women.

As I have been working on this book, colleagues and friends have asked me, usually with a glint in their eye, "Well, what did you find out?" The glint, I have assumed, invited me to make a brash statement that would lead to spirited debate. Yet the only true conclusion I could offer is that women are complicated. Men, no doubt, are too. In this book, I invite those interested in women's development to meet the women I have studied and to ponder with me.

Acknowledgments

Over the years, a great many people have given their time and their intelligence to this work. Much of the information for the first phase of the study was collected for my doctoral dissertation. I received enormous support, insight, and guidance from my teacher and mentor, Joseph Adelson. Other members of my thesis committee, particularly Fredrick Wyatt and the late Selma Fraiberg, contributed their wisdom to the underpinnings of this work. I am grateful to June Price and Susan Schenkel for their perceptive commentary on the individual college-age protocols.

The Faculty Research Committee of Towson State University was generous in providing travel funds for interviewing during the second phase of data collection. But this project was completed without a large grant. Without the diligence and investment of my students, the follow-up study would never have taken place. They learned the art of detective work in tracing the subjects, organized the data, helped me design and pilot the follow-up questionnaire, participated in the interviewing, and helped with literature reviews. Special thanks to Megan Bell, Priscilla Dorsey, Ana de la Macorra, Pattrice Maurer, Stephanie

Saunders, and Sharon Weiss. I also thank Janis Carlos for secretarial support beyond the call of duty.

My friends and colleagues provided the inspiration and motivation necessary to assist me in completing work on this project. They also read early drafts of the manuscript and made insightful and helpful comments. I am grateful to Judith Armstrong, Jerrold Post, Barbara Sadick, Pam Sheff, and Irvin Yalom for providing a general support group for the book—and for me.

My deepest thanks go to the women who are the subject of this book. They spoke to me, a stranger, with openness and feeling and contributed their time and energy for no return. I hope that I do them justice in this work and that their life stories can teach others some portion of what they taught me.

Baltimore, Maryland   Ruthellen Josselson
June 1987

The Author

Ruthellen Josselson received her Ph.D. degree (1972) in clinical psychology from the University of Michigan. She has been a clinical instructor in psychiatry at the Harvard University Medical School, associate research scientist at the Johns Hopkins University, and assistant professor of psychology at the University of Toledo. Currently, she is both a practicing psychotherapist and associate professor of psychology at Towson State University. Her research and published articles have focused on clarifying normal developmental processes in adolescence.

To my mother,
Anne Lederman Lefkowitz,
with love

Finding
Herself

What thou lovest well remains
　　the rest is dross
What thou lov'st well shall not be reft from thee
What thou lov'st well is thy true heritage
Whose world, or mine or theirs
　　or is it of none?

　　　　　　　　—Ezra Pound, *Canto LXXXI*

Chapter 1

Woman:
A Modern Sphinx

> If you want to know more about femininity, enquire from your own experiences of life, or turn to the poets, or wait until science can give you deeper and more coherent information.
> —*Sigmund Freud, "Femininity"*

Isabel, Katherine, and Jane attended the same university during the late 1960s and early 1970s. Although they never met each other, they witnessed together the crumbling of the social barriers that restricted women's life choices. While they were coming of age, the rising voice of feminism preached that all things were possible for women. Choosing how they would live their lives became a serious and complicated task; the fetters that determined life for previous generations of women no longer bound this one.

When I interviewed Isabel in college, she was in the midst of an identity crisis. "I'm in the middle of two societies, a liberal one and a very, very strict one. I don't think I can decide—ever," she said. Twelve years later, at the age of thirty-three, Isabel has all but forgotten her adolescent anguish and is happily committed to a "best friend" of a husband, two children, and a part-time nursing job. From the plethora of choices available to her, she chose what best fit herself. In short, she constructed an identity. Katherine, who had prided herself on her intellectual

1

achievements in college while being a rebellious hippie, regrets, at age thirty-four, never having found a man to marry, but devotes herself to her legal career, her friends, and her parrot—also happily. Jane seemed not to notice the social upheaval surrounding her in college. She remained committed to her family's religious values, realized her childhood dream of becoming an elementary schoolteacher, and, at age thirty-three, continues to find happiness in her teaching career, her religion, and the new family she has created with her husband.

Three women, together in the same historical moment, chose three different lives. Their differences caution us against our current social tendency to generalize about "all" women. Their "ordinariness" stands in sharp contrast to the media image of the modern woman. Trying to understand how these women came to the choices they made is a complicated endeavor and one that occupied me for seventeen years.

Years ago, women who submitted to their husband's decision making, who raised the children, canned the fruit, cleaned the house, and had orgasms regularly would have been viewed by psychology (as well as society) as approximating ideal womanhood. In those days, women who wanted to assert themselves or realize their individuality were often diagnosed as neurotic, suffering from penis envy and nonacceptance of the female role. Now the pendulum has swung to the other side, and we expect women to be self-actualizing and independent. Our folk heroines are women who transcend marriage and succeed in business. Our literature now focuses on how to make women more assertive or independent. Relationship is out; achievement is in. Or women labor under the ideal of being superwoman: a star at the office, devoted mother and wife at home, and in prime physical shape.

Throughout history, a woman's place has been defined by her society. Even when these definitions are more implicit than explicit, women are susceptible to cultural definitions of how they ought to be and sensitive to social guidelines that tell them whether they are doing a good job at being women. In the middle of the 1960s, to plan to have a career was considered anything from unrealistic to neurotic to avant-garde. I recall presenting some "new" feminist ideas to an undergraduate introductory psychology class in 1968. The students laughed at the idea of women having serious achievement goals. Who would raise the children? they wanted to know. By the late 1970s, women who raised families in lieu of paid employment felt denigrated and defensive. College women today assume that if they do not find careers they will have to explain themselves to all manner of protesting others. None would dare admit to being in college to find a husband, although some are. Meanwhile, popular magazines are beginning to report that women "have it all" only at the cost of much anxiety, guilt, stress, and exhaustion, and women are beginning to leave executive positions to be with children at home. The pendulum seems to be swinging once again.

Within the parameters dictated by the social climate, each woman nevertheless makes choices about what best fits her own goals and wishes for a life. Even in the most restrictive society, there is some avenue for self-expression. Perhaps no group of women has ever had quite as much latitude for such individual choice as have women born in the United States since World War II. Men no longer define women. The elusive goal of self-definition is within a woman's grasp. What do I want? is a question that each woman decides for herself. The process of deciding what she most deeply wants coincides with the formation of her identity.

The most important developmental task facing women today is the formation of identity, for it is in the realm of identity that a woman bases her sense of herself as well as her vision of the structure of her life. Identity incorporates a woman's choices for herself, her priorities, and the guiding principles by which she makes decisions. How does a woman come to form an identity? How does a woman determine what she most deeply wants?

Freud never reached a satisfactory answer to his question of what a woman wants. For him, women seemed too fluid, shifting, intangible, amoral, unprincipled, and indeterminate. Women have since foiled several generations of psychological researchers, whose neat, ordered theories of developmental pri-

orities and developmental stages founder and fall in the face of
female inscrutability.

Beginning with Freud, and ever since, the psychoanalytic
theory of human development has been conceived in terms of
male development, with female development either ignored,
treated as an afterthought, or forced into parallel lines of rea-
soning. Previous research, in its effort to append the understanding of women to existing understanding of men, has largely overlooked the dominant issues in female development: issues
of interpersonal relatedness, for example, and the role of affiliation in the quest for meaning in life. Only recently have women
theorists begun to address female needs for attachment and connection to others, pointing the way toward a new set of concepts with which to make sense out of the course of development in women (Chodorow, 1978; Gilligan, 1982; Miller, 1976;
Belenky and others, 1986).

Women and Other Women

Psychologists and sociologists have fervently pursued the
question of how and why women differ from men. Answers to
this question have created an amalgam of generalizations about
women, some insightful, some tautological, and some specious.
(Maccoby and Jacklin, 1974, and Bernard, 1974, offer critical
reviews of the sex-differences literature.)

The easiest thing to do in psychological research is to find
a sex difference. On almost any personality variable, given a
large enough sample, the sexes will differ in a statistically significant way. This result occurs partly because men and women
differ, but even more because the statistical means differ. Take,
for example, a variable such as independence. If one constructs
a personality measure of independence and uses a large enough
sample, one might find that 52 percent of the men and 48 percent of the women are high in independence. This difference is
large enough not to be likely to arise by chance, and therefore
the researcher may conclude that men are significantly more independent than women. The degree of overlap—that is, the percentage of men and women who score similarly on the test—is

almost never reported in the psychological literature. We therefore can say some things about how the average woman may
differ from the average man, but, in doing this, we omit consideration of the enormous variance of any trait within each sex.

Whether boys and girls, men and women differ from each
other will be a subject of ongoing debate. But in phrasing our
question this way, we are forced to assume that women as a
group and men as a group are internally coherent. The consideration of sex differences will not be pursued in this work,
largely because I do not believe that it has illuminated our
knowledge about women. The finding, for example, that wom-
en are less aggressive and more dependent than men (Bernard,
1974) tells us little about the important dimensions or organization of female personality. It allows us no insight into Isabel,
Katherine, and Jane.

We have long taken it for granted that men differ from
each other in important ways worthy of careful study and
understanding. But we have rather assumed that all women are
fundamentally alike. In our understanding of women's development we have lacked perspective on the different pathways to
development as a woman, the different roads a girl may travel
on the way to womanhood. In fact, personality and life-course
differences among women may be the most important bits of
evidence for building an understanding of the crucial dimensions of female development. What we need are meaningful
ways to compare women with each other. Yet we are not sure
which are the centrally important dimensions, especially with a
culture that is so uncertain about these matters.

The available work that compares women to one another
generally does so on variables chosen because of their political
significance. Thus, we have comparisons of homemakers and career women (for example, Stewart, 1980; Mellinger and Erdwins, 1985; Hall and Gordon, 1973; Ferree, 1984), working
mothers and homemakers (for example, Lortie-Lussier, Schwab,
and de Koninck, 1985), feminists and nonfeminists (for example, Johnson and others, 1981), lesbians and heterosexuals (for
example, Oberstone, 1976). But these dimensions, in that they
are specific contents of a larger identity, may be only superficial

or transient. They may not represent the integrity of the individual; they do not tell us who a woman most deeply is or how she organizes herself as a whole person. This research tradition has taught us something about women's parts. It has told us little about how the parts are fitted together into some meaningful whole.

Another major source of information about women has been clinical psychologists and psychoanalysts. Struggling to be helpful to their women patients, female clinicians have taken the opportunity to define issues that emerge as pivotal and shared among women (Eichenbaum and Orbach, 1983; Kaplan and Klein, 1985; Stiver, 1984; Kaplan, 1986). Feminist therapists have served to correct and counterbalance the androcentricity of psychoanalytic theory as well as to illuminate aspects of female development that remained outside the purview of psychoanalytic thought.

Yet, to deduce a normative theory of women from the data of psychopathology only perpetuates the much-criticized tendency of psychoanalysis to assume isomorphism between the anguish of the consulting room and patterns of ongoing, normal human growth. An adequate understanding of women will wed the depth of the psychoanalytic tradition to observations of people who are living their lives in what they consider to be a satisfactory manner.

Women are not all alike, although they may be alike in some ways. Women differ from each other in ways beyond their roles. The most important differences among women lie in internal personality configurations, not between those who are "just" mothers and those who are corporate executives. A consideration of identity formation offers a means of beginning to differentiate women from each other. If we think of identity formation as a process and not a content, as Erik Erikson did, we can look at different pathways to different forms of identity. Here we are interested not in discriminating women who choose careers from those who choose only to raise families but rather in understanding the differences between women who have attained a solid and reliable sense of identity and those whose identities are more precarious. A homemaker and a woman who is a corporate president can have equally well-formulated identities. In looking at identity formation as a process, we can step outside societal debates about the role of women and also keep apart from the influence of political consciousness. The consolidation of identity is an aspect of good, healthy personality development whatever its contents. The study of how women go about this task will yield perspective both on the nature of female development and on the meaningful dimensions that underlie differences among women.

Women differ in how much they are willing or able to explore possibilities within themselves, how much they realize their individuality and uniqueness, and how much they allow themselves to be defined by others. In this book, we will explore these differences in the lives of individual women. Some women adopt life projects that have been passed to them through their families. For the sake of brevity, we will call such women *Foreclosures*. (See Chapter Three for a complete discussion of the definitions of the groups and derivations of the labels.) Other women, those we will term *Identity Diffusions*, treat themselves as lumps of clay available to be shaped by whatever or whoever is willing to mold them. Still others actively and consciously test possible ways of being in an effort to discover an identity that fits their inner selves—the *Moratoriums*. Those women who eventually formulate an identity, who seek cultural avenues to express their sense of themselves, and who make commitments to ways of being and experiencing we will call *Identity Achievements*. This book uses these women's stories to explore psychological development in women or, more precisely, to develop a theory of development in a language and from a vantage point useful to the understanding of women. Its starting point is a quest for the phenomenology that must be the basis of a psychology of women.

This book is also about a particular transitional period of development, the passage from adolescence to adulthood, a time in which crucial identity choices are made. By following women's lives from adolescence through early adulthood, this book will show the pathways that lead to identity formation. Identity formation, in the psychosocial sense defined by Erikson, is the developmental task attempted at adolescence that links the newly autonomous individual to society. Identity is the interface between the individual and the world, defining as it does what the individual will stand for and be recognized as. Although the study of identity formation in men has been a relatively straightforward inquiry, the study of identity formation in women has been fraught with ambiguity and frustration. Men are wont to define themselves by occupation or by their distinctiveness from others, which makes their identity easy to name. Women, by contrast, orient themselves in more complicated ways, balancing many involvements and aspirations, with connections to others paramount; their identities are thus compounded and more difficult to articulate.

At the close of adolescence, the identity work accomplished appears to have profound implications for the remainder of the life course—perhaps particularly so for women. Decisions about marriage, career, or children will, for example, either constrain or engender later choices (Stewart, 1980; Rossi, 1980). Adolescence, then, becomes a critical time for sketching the parameters of adult roles. The development that occurs in adolescence in turn depends on previous personality development. Ego development and childhood conflict resolution are important precursors of identity formation.

Subjects chosen for this study were college seniors, women at the threshold of their adulthood whose developmental task was the resolution of some fundamental identity issues. At the time I first studied them, I was trying to understand the psychodynamic and developmental roots of their differing modes of identity resolution or nonresolution. The tendency among those of us who do research on identity formation with college students is to assume that those who seem to have resolved identity matters at the close of college will follow a smooth course and that those who fail at identity resolution will continue to have difficulty. Only one previous study, using a male sample, has investigated the longer-term effects of identity resolution in college (Marcia, 1976).

To test this assumption, I recontacted the women I had previously studied ten to twelve years later in order to learn about the impact that late-adolescent identity resolution had on the now-adult women. Intensive interviews at two important points in their lives allowed me to observe clearly the changes in their orientations to their lives over time. Memory has a way of making the past consistent with the present as people amend their ongoing autobiographies. Studying women as they are becoming adults and again as adulthood is in progress sheds light on how the critical decision making of identity formation during the late-adolescent period determines the shape and rhythm of the early adulthood years. With observation at these two points in time, we can see factors operating that the women themselves are often unaware of or cannot articulate. We have access to the consistency in their lives and in their psychological make-up as well as to the changes.

This book is inhabited by happy people, people who are at least contented with their lives, who are "making it" in a way that leads them, at least, not to define themselves as having problems. Clinical psychologists are much more accustomed to understanding the roots of troubles; we know less about the ingredients that make for harmonious adjustment. At the same time, the women who are to be introduced are happy in somewhat different ways. Different choices bring different gratifications, challenges, and struggles.

Chapter 2

Becoming Herself:
Identity, Individuation,
and Intimacy

A woman's whole life is a history of the affections.
—*Washington Irving,* "The Broken Heart"

Identity is a word that has been much overused, in many contexts, to mean many things. It is necessary, then, to take care to consider carefully what this term encompasses. Erikson (1950, 1956, 1958, 1968, 1975) has been our most important theorist of identity. He was responsible for the notion of the *identity crisis* and drew attention, with richly detailed writing, ιo the importance of this aspect of personality. Most fundamentally, he defined identity as a primarily unconscious process that unites personality and links the individual to the social world. As a crucial aspect of the self, identity serves the individual in a variety of ways.

Identity is the stable, consistent, and reliable sense of who one is and what one stands for in the world. It integrates one's meaning to oneself and one's meaning to others; it provides a match between what one regards as central to oneself and how one is viewed by significant others in one's life.

Identity is also a way of preserving the continuity of the self, linking the past and the present. In states of identity diffu-

10

sion, a person experiences a sense of not knowing who she or he is and feels at the mercy of parts of the self, impulses, memories, and traits that do not add up or feel coherently connected to a core self. In its essence, identity becomes a means by which people organize and understand their experience and deeply share their meaning systems with others. What we choose to value and deprecate, our system of ethics—these form the core of our sense of identity.

At the same time that our identity is fundamentally interwoven with others' to gain meaning, contrasting ourselves with others heightens our sense of what is uniquely individual. Often, we learn who we are by discovering our differences from others, by finding out how we may distinguish ourselves from those we feel most like. A young woman I knew told of how she came to learn that she had special musical talent. One day in second-grade music class, the teacher was trying to help students understand the concept of musical intervals. My friend, however, simply named the notes. "That's a G and a D," she said. The teacher, astonished, began playing other notes for her to identify, and each time the child named the note correctly. The teacher told her that she had perfect pitch. Now it was my friend's turn to be astonished. "Doesn't everyone?" she asked.

Identity thus becomes a way of judging ourselves with respect to a typology or set of values that is meaningful to others with whom we identify ourselves. Within a professional community, for example, each person has some idea of how she or he fits and understands that peers respond to the same nuances of accomplishment, recognition, and status that the group deems significant in evaluating others. Outside this community, one may be known simply as, for example, a doctor, and be responded to and evaluated by a different set of standards.

Identity Formation

Over the course of a life, particularly as the circle of significant others and meaningful activities widens, identity is continually refined. The process of identity formation takes place throughout the life cycle, beginning just after birth as we gradually become aware that we have a self, continuing to old age, when we come to terms with the meaning that self has expressed in the larger scheme of things.

In psychodynamic terms, identity is neither a structure nor a content but a property of the ego that organizes experience. It is an amalgam, according to Erikson, of constitutional givens, idiosyncratic libidinal needs, psychological defenses against inner conflict, significant identifications with important others, interests, and social roles. In a sense, we might think of identity formation as the assembling of a jigsaw puzzle in which each person has somewhat different pieces to fit together. Natural talents, intelligence, social class, physical attractiveness, genetic aspects of temperament, physical limitations, early deprivation, and traumatic experience all render a unique hue to the identity-formation task.

Erikson showed that although identity is formed through identification with others who come to have meaning to us, identity is greater than the sum of these past identifications. Adults as well as children identify with aspects of people who matter to them, who are admired or powerful. Identity formation is the work of transforming and assembling these identifications into a coherent whole with a center that holds. As a mechanism, identification has limited usefulness because a child identifies with only parts of others, and these part identifications do not add up to a fully functioning person. A woman may enjoy cooking as her mother does and be interested in baseball like her father, but these two interests do not make an identity for her. They are pieces of a self; we know nothing about her identity unless we know where these pieces fit in the overall picture she creates.

Identity includes, but supersedes, all previous identities. Choosing an identity is not like choosing a college: there is no one day when it happens. Rather, the self is gradually modified so that one day one may look back and realize that one has changed inexorably, that one is different from how one used to be and is still essentially the same.

Identity, then, is a dynamic fitting together of parts of the personality with the realities of the social world so that a person has a sense both of internal coherence and meaningful relatedness to the real world. To say, for example, "I am a psychologist" is a statement of occupational identity, but it does not define the overall identity unless all that one is is subsumed under being-a-psychologist. Even to say "I am a woman, a mother, and a psychologist" does not define identity because it merely lists aspects of an identity and gives no information about how these parts are synthesized or how the person experiences herself.

Social role is just one aspect of identity, although, being the most visible, it is most available for study. We do not yet understand how identity changes as social roles fluctuate or whether social roles are derived from identity. Clearly, some people have always been able to create social roles for themselves out of a strong sense of whom they wished to be. They have, as Erikson put it, caused society to adapt to them. Others—most people, in fact—are likely to choose a social role from those that their society offers readily.

Identity, in contrast to social role, is largely unconscious. Once formulated, it allows us to function almost automatically, without our having to ponder each of the thousands of choices made in a single day. With a smoothly functioning identity, we can take ourselves for granted as being who we are. Erikson, in elaborating this paradox, said that we are most aware of our identity when we are just about to make its acquaintance. This period of meeting our identity he called the *Moratorium phase,* but it has come to be generally known as the *identity crisis.* In such a period, we are most aware of our choices, most likely to be imagining or experimenting with alternative selves. We realize that we do not have to continue to be as we have been; we consider revisions and try out our new possibilities on others to discover their reactions. Once identity decisions are made, the questioning and dilemmas fade and in their place comes peace of mind in a sense of purposefulness and an inner expectation of mutuality with those who matter to us.

In Erikson's depiction of the life cycle, identity resolution is a stage-specific normative crisis that takes place at adolescence. His schematic representation of the life cycle and his

discussion of the stages of life show that although issues related
to identity have been in preparation before adolescence and will
continue to be refined and reworked after, at adolescence issues
of identity take center stage. Before adolescence, much that re-
lates to identity is ascribed: one's social class, whom one must
live with and get along with, what school one attends, what religion one practices. In earlier, less complicated times or in other, simpler, less diverse cultures, identity remains ascribed
through the life cycle. A person is born to a place in society,
and development consists of learning the roles and molding the
self that is appropriate to this prearranged social niche. In our
present, highly diverse cultural milieu, where one may do and
be many things, one must make choices in order to formulate
one's identity. At the close of adolescence the first choices are
made. As adolescence ends, the young person carves out a place
in the world, and society identifies the person as responsible
for choices made. The tentativeness with which society regards
college students gives way to the labels (*teacher, married, conservative*) awarded the young adult.

　　Recognizing the importance of this growth process, complex societies make available to the young person a moratorium,
a period of delay in which it is understood that the person will
not yet be taken quite seriously. Society grants permission to
the adolescent to play at adulthood, to try on roles, to experiment with selves. At the end of this period, society expects and
more or less ceremonializes commitments, formalizing its intention to regard the young person as being in earnest.

　　The adolescent in today's world is poignantly aware of
the necessity of making choices, and much of adolescence is oriented toward experimentation with possibilities, trial assumption of roles, testing of capacity in order to find choices that fit
the givens of the self. Once choices have been made and synthesized, the resultant identity becomes a template for the making
of adult decisions. As the life cycle progresses, identity becomes
amplified and differentiated, often fundamentally modified, but
it can never be undone. Choices made become part of the individual's history. Previous identity must always be integrated
with the new. The identity-formation period, then, is a critical
time. It is the hatching period of the adult.

Although identity formation is the major developmental task of adolescence, especially late adolescence, it is not a readily observable drama. The process of identity formation tends to occur gradually, incrementally, often unintentionally. It is Aristotelian in inevitability but not in drama. Identity comprises inconspicuous as well as deliberate choices. Whom one chooses for friends, what one reads or does not read, whether one learns to play tennis or oboe, whether one takes drugs or not—all these choices both reflect an ongoing sense of identity and influence the identity that will emerge. Even the protagonists of the identity-formation drama, the young people themselves, are unaware of the script of the play. In living through the Moratorium period, they may make sincere commitments and think they "mean it," only to learn later on that they were only experimenting, only stopping at a way station.

Erikson's concept of identity was a major contribution to psychological theory as well as the impetus for studying post-childhood stages of development. The term *identity crisis* became popular and was applied to every form of distress from age twelve on, with much loss to the subtlety and nuance of Erikson's work. Nevertheless, Erikson made it clear that much that happens during adolescence influences the future life course through the identity process, and his work spurred interest in discovering how this process occurs.

Erikson views the impetus for identity formation at adolescence to be a convergence of epigenetic and social forces, but he does not link this development to a larger psychodynamic consideration of adolescent growth. His concept of identity subsumes Peter Blos's (1962) concept of consolidation, integration, and ego continuity and Kernberg's (1976) stress on the capacity for total object relations as major tasks of adolescent development.

Blos (1967) emphasizes the centrality of separation-individuation as a precursor to identity formation. Adolescent development achieves the sharpening of boundaries and clarification of attributes of the self that are distinct from others. "Individuation implies that the growing person takes increasing responsibility for what he does and what he is rather than depositing this responsibility on the shoulders of those under

whose influence and tutelage he has grown up" (p. 168). Blos's
concept of successful individuation at adolescence bears much
resemblance to Erikson's concept of identity.

In order to understand identity formation, then, we are
led to consider processes of separation-individuation. Individuation, autonomy, and identity formation are linked. As aspects
of the self are freed from an array of primitive, narcissistic, and
totalistic identifications, autonomous ego functions become
available for identity formation. Therefore, one cannot understand an individual identity without considering the psychic
mass from which that identity precipitates.

Separation-Individuation

Identity formation in adolescence expands on the earliest
efforts to cope with the fact of separateness and the conflicts
that separateness entails. The ego that undertakes the adolescent task was formed in the resolution of the early childhood
problem of connection and autonomy. Paradoxical needs for
self-assertion and union, with their accompanying dangers of
isolation and annihilation, continue throughout the life cycle.

Mahler's (Mahler, Pine, and Bergman, 1975) theory of
separation-individuation traces the earliest emergence of the
sense of identity. In the beginning of psychological life, there
is no self. The newborn infant, as best we can understand it, experiences pleasure and pain but has no sense of an "I" that is
doing that experiencing. By the age of three years, the young
child has developed a firm sense of self-boundaries, knows clearly that he or she is a person separate from other people with
unique thoughts and inner experiences.

Earliest infancy is a period in which mother and infant
are fused, from the infant's point of view. This symbiotic mass
is sometimes pleasurable and sometimes painful, but the infant
is not aware that there is a separate and distinct mother who is
or is not gratifying. In the initial subphase of separation-individuation, differentiation, the baby has the first inklings of separate self and other (object). This is a hatching phase, to use
Mahler's word, in which the infant begins dimly to perceive that

certain experiences originate from inside the body and others from outside.

Locomotion, and with it the ability to move away from mother, initiates the second subphase, practicing. In this period, babies become intoxicated with their own increasing cognitive and motor abilities, want to explore everything, and believe themselves to be omnipotent and capable of magic. Babies are most likely to explore their world in optimal proximity to their mothers, needing their mothers near while proving that they do not need their mothers at all. By the late days of the practicing subphase, babies have moved far from the engulfment of earliest infancy but are near enough to it to fear merging once more. Awareness and experience of selfhood are still new and fragile, must be asserted and guarded from the dangers of becoming again a part of mother.

By eighteen months, toddlers have the cognitive capacity to be aware of the separateness they have achieved from mother, and this awareness gives rise to an increased preoccupation with her. Mahler calls this third subphase rapprochement because children are beginning to attempt to integrate their needs for closeness to mother with their needs for independence from her. "At the very height of mastery, toward the end of the practicing period, it had already begun to dawn on the junior toddler that the world is not his oyster, that he must cope with it more or less 'on his own,' very often as a relatively helpless, small, and separate individual, unable to command relief or assistance merely by feeling the need for it or even by giving voice to that need" (Mahler, Pine, and Bergman, 1975, p. 78). In other words, the full impact of separateness comes upon toddlers during the rapprochement subphase. Separation is not just the joyfulness and freedom that they thought it was. It also implies aloneness, helplessness, and overwhelming danger. During the rapprochement subphase, toddlers demand their mothers' investment in the autonomy experienced during the practicing phase. They wish to share the new experiences but also have an increased need for their mothers' love.

The rapprochement subphase is one of the most critical and difficult, for both mothers and children, in all of early development. Because children are experiencing conflicting needs for both autonomy and connection at the same time, they are vulnerable to massive distortions in psychic development if the intensity of need or the reactions of mother overwhelm the fragile ego organization. A mother too ready to reexperience the symbiosis of early infancy may discourage the autonomy of her toddler in favor of renewed clinging behavior. Or a mother too relieved to be past the relative merging of infancy may be too unavailable for the renewed neediness her child expresses.

Spanning the ages of roughly eighteen months to three years, the rapprochement subphase encompasses the period when the most important internalizations occur, internalizations that form the building blocks for all later development. In order to cope with the complexities of the rapprochement stage, the child begins, more and more, to make what is external part of the self. Introjection, taking in a part of the parent as part of the self, also frees the child from excessive dependence on the parents. If a little girl can soothe and comfort herself as her mother always did, she is thereby freed somewhat from her reliance on her mother. This soothing, comforting aspect of mother, through the process of introjection, is now part of herself. Because fear of the loss of love makes its appearance during this subphase, children also internalize parental demands as part of themselves, as protection from possible transgressions. In psychoanalytic terms, these demands or rules form the basis of the superego, an internal parent that keeps the child from being "bad" and getting punished. Similarly, mechanisms of identification, or becoming like the parents, help to defend the child against increased feelings of vulnerability during this stage. Because parents are experienced as omnipotent and children are increasingly aware of their own vulnerability, an effort to become like the parent is in the service of regaining omnipotence.

The outcome of the rapprochement subphase is the capacity to function separately, made possible by the gradual internalization of aspects of the object world. If development in this subphase proceeds adequately, the child will have internalized a constant, positive image of mother so that mother can be envisioned and sensed even when she is not present. With a constant and reliable inner image of mother, the child can tolerate separation from her despite tension or need. With separation-individuation on its way to completion, the child develops a sense of individuality, a core of selfhood on which all later identity formation is based.

The latency phase, the period between childhood and adolescence, roughly spanning ages six to twelve, reaps the benefits of the conflict resolution of childhood. The child is, throughout this phase, both realistically and emotionally dependent on the parents but has a separate sense of self. The superego, which is composed primarily of parental representations, is in harmony with the actual parents. Child and parents have the same sense of what is good and bad, what is to be valued and not. Self-esteem is derived largely from parental approval and the growth of skills, generally skills chosen by or at least aided by the parents. Belief in parental omnipotence is intact during this stage, and much of the child's continuing growth rests on increasing identification with parental ego functions.

The harmony of the latency phase is shattered by the instinctual surge of puberty and the psychosocially induced demands for further separation from the parents. As in the earlier rapprochement subphase of development, the adolescent wants both to move away from parents and to stay near them to feel safe. Increasing autonomy and mobility involve the adolescent more deeply in the extrafamilial world. Peers and other admired people begin to absorb some of the emotional energy formerly reserved for parents.

Much of the early theory of adolescent development conceptualized adolescence as a period in which psychological independence was won by detachment and replacement of parents as important objects (Freud, 1958; Fountain, 1961; Blos, 1962). Mounting research evidence, however, led to a revision in that theory as it became clear that adolescents do not abandon or disown their parents as a necessary condition for growth (Douvan and Adelson, 1966; Offer, 1969; Offer, Ostrov, and Howard, 1981). Separation-individuation in adolescence requires a revision of relationships with parents, a revision that nevertheless preserves connection.

Many adolescents are unable to individuate from their internal parents because they were never able to live up to what they thought their parents wanted of them. In anger, they may try to leave home, but because the parents are inside of them, they find themselves, in the end, unable to get away. They remain eternally dissatisfied with themselves, endlessly trying to please or refusing to please their internalized parents, from whom they are unable to emancipate themselves.

Separation, then, does not imply individuation. Nor is physical separation necessary for individuation. Many young people become their own person without ever leaving home. What is critical here is that aspects of the self become reworked during adolescence so that the young person has some choice in the creation of a self, a self that will function autonomously but in relation to the parents.

Once again, a rapprochement process appears to be important. When a new element of self is formed, it tends to be tested, at least in fantasy, in the context of the parents from whom the young person is individuating (Josselson, 1980). A young woman choosing her first formal dress is more likely to imagine what her parents will think of her in it than what her date will think. Will they see her as grown up, feminine? Will they respond to her emerging womanhood or think of her as a child playing dress-up?

Or we might think of the young college woman who becomes involved with a religion very different from her family's. What will they think of this? Should she tell them of her activities? How will she handle their disapproval? This is an internal debate, a discussion with parents who are inside the self, who seem to be insisting that one may not change, may not be different and still be loved. The challenge of this developmental phase is to gain a feeling of individuality in the context of an ongoing relationship to parents.

Throughout adolescence, individuation proceeds through gradual accretions of competence, with the young person gradually taking over functions formerly provided by parents. From learning to drive, earning and managing spending money, turning to peers for emotional support, and other such rites of passage, adolescents increase their reliance on their own capacities, with parents more or less in the background, to be relied on in times of need or distress. As the adolescent individuates, gaining autonomy from parents, those aspects that are liberated within the personality are available to be recombined into new ways of experiencing the self.

Separation-individuation thus does not abolish relationship; rather, it requires revision of relationship. To fully understand development during the identity-formation stage, therefore, we must look at both sides of the process: both the individuating, autonomous part and the connecting/relating self.

Identity is always bound to one's sense of connection to others. From its earliest roots, identity emerges from what is separated out from others but continues to exist in connection with them. Identity fuses into a creative, emergent whole the sense of who one was (with whom) and the sense of who one will be (with whom). Identity formation is not necessarily cataclysmic; it may rest on modulation and selective acceptance of how one has always been (Schafer, 1973). Rejection and behavior change are only more dramatic than modulation.

Identity, then, is neither the sum of roles nor an intrapsychic process alone. Nor is it who one is for others or who one is apart from others. It is all these things. Socialization theories have tended to focus on social roles as they exist apart from personality development. To that extent, these theories depict rootless beings taking a place in the world. Psychoanalytic theory has tended to view personality development as wholly internal, disconnected to the larger psychosocial world, and, as a result, cannot account for the nature of the investments that become central in adult development. But to keep both intrapsychic aspects of development and psychosocial demands and interests clearly in focus at the same time is an extraordinarily challenging task. Because these streams converge most visibly in identity formation, we will attempt to view identity formation as both an intrapsychic and a psychosocial process.

Thus far, we have defined identity and looked at the developmental processes that underlie separation-individuation. We have seen how these concepts converge in the notion that identity always emerges from a matrix of past selves, where the earliest sense of self crystalizes out of a merged, symbiotic attachment to mother. With development, in a context of ongoing relationships, aspects of the self that were tied to internalized parents become freed for new investments. How these new investments are organized and reworked becomes the cornerstone of adult identity.

Intimacy

In Erikson's (1950, 1956, 1968) eight-stage depiction of the life cycle, issues of identity must be resolved before issues of the next stage, intimacy versus isolation, are addressed. One must have decided who and what one is and will be before attempting the interconnection of identities that is intimacy.

At this point in his writing, it becomes most apparent that Erikson, like Freud and most other important psychological theorists, is writing about men. Indeed, all Erikson's psychobiographies analyze identity as it develops in men, and most of his case examples are from male patients. All Erikson had to say about women was that much of a woman's identity resides in her choice of the men she wants to be sought by (1968). Here Erikson suggests that intimacy may precede identity for a woman—that is, a woman cannot define who she is until she chooses who she will be in relation to her mate-to-be.

Influenced by Erikson's conceptualization, researchers concluded that indeed intimacy seems to precede or at least be contemporaneous with identity among adolescent girls and young women (Douvan and Adelson, 1966; Orlofsky, 1977; Josselson, Greenberger, and McConochie, 1977; Marcia, 1980; Hodgson and Fischer, 1981; Morgan, 1982). Debates and disputes about this formulation, especially with the advent of feminist researchers, have, however, been vociferous.

A major difficulty in resolving this conundrum is that no one has as yet looked seriously at how identity is organized in women. Recent work seems to suggest that the question of whether identity precedes, follows, or commingles with developmental issues of intimacy may itself be a poorly conceived one.

Perhaps our psychological theory of development has been a theory of separation and autonomy rather than a theory of connection and relationship (Miller, 1976; Surrey, 1984). Perhaps a central aspect of identity is the commitment to a self-in-relation rather than to a self that stands alone facing an abstract world. Reconceptualized this way, the life stages for women are perhaps different from those for men.

We know little about female adolescents, in that much of the theory of adolescence has been written to describe male phenomena (Adelson and Doehrman, 1980). We do know, however, that interpersonal competence is more important to adolescent girls than is autonomy and that girls are less likely than boys to separate forcefully from parents (Coleman, 1961; Douvan and Adelson, 1966; Josselson, Greenberger, and McConochie, 1977). In short, adolescent girls seem to formulate identity more in connection to others and at less distance from their families than do boys.

Recently, researchers and theoreticians have raised a converging complaint that concepts of autonomy, independence, and abstract achievement do not describe the focal issues of growing up female. Gilligan's (1982) influential study of moral development showed that women conceptualize and experience the world "in a different voice," a voice that is more person centered and empathic, more emotionally connected and less abstract than the male voice. Men and women, concludes Gilligan, operate with different internal models. Where a dominant image for men is that of hierarchy, competition to be alone at the top, women respond to their lives through the image of the web, or concerns about connectedness. For men, wishing to be alone at the top, the fear is that others will get too close, that they will be caught and diminished. For women, wishing to be at the center of connection, the dominant fear is of being stranded, far out on the edge and isolated from others. As a result of these pervasive and fundamental differences, experiences such as achievement and affiliation are different for men and women, even though behavioral manifestations may look similar.

Others (Belenky and others, 1986) have taken these observations further and suggested that women have unique, intuitive means of knowing that are silenced when value is placed only on logic and symbol. Women's epistemological sense is rooted in connecting reality to an ongoing sense of self; the objective is imbued with the subjective. To know is to connect with rather than to master.

Chodorow (1978) argues that women, because they are mothered by someone of the same sex, form a different inner patterning of relationships that prevents them from ever becoming as separate as men. "From the retention of preoedipal attachments to their mother, growing girls come to define and experience themselves as continuous with others; their experience of self contains more flexible or permeable ego boundaries. Boys come to define themselves as more separate and distinct, with a greater sense of rigid ego boundaries and differentiation. The basic feminine sense of self is connected to the world; the basic masculine sense of self is separate" (p. 169). Experimental evidence (Aries and Olver, 1985) corroborates Chodorow's view that female infants, in contrast to males, develop with less separateness from mothers.

Working in a different context and with quite different data, May (1980) came to similar conclusions. His search for universal myths that underlie male and female consciousness led him to much the same phenomena as Chodorow and Gilligan found. May looked at fantasy productions of men and women to understand the central motifs or themes that might represent organizing inner mythologies. For men, the archetypal myth is the story of Phaëthon, a tale of ambition, striving, and failure. For women, the archetypal myth is the story of Demeter and Persephone: love, loss, and reunion. May concluded that men organize themselves, at a psychologically deep level, around the axis of achievement and failure (May calls this pattern *Pride*), while women are centered on themes of separation and connection (*Caring*).

Miller and her research group (Miller, 1976, 1984; Kaplan and Klein, 1985; Surrey, 1984) have been positing the existence of a "relational self" in women that is central to their growth. "Development according to the male model overlooks the fact that women's development is proceeding but on another basis.

. . . Indeed, women's sense of self becomes very much organized around being able to make and then to maintain affiliations and relationships" (Miller, 1976, p. 83).

All these writers share a growing recognition of the importance of relatedness to women and the necessity of finding some psychological constructs to describe its growth and vicissitudes.

Erikson wrestled with this question in his much-debated paper "Womanhood and Inner Space" (1968). Using but modifying Freud's "anatomy is destiny" dictum, Erikson's metaphor of the inner space calls attention to feminine modes of perceiving reality. Although this paper is frequently cited negatively by feminist writers (see Erikson, 1975), Erikson, in his characteristically complex style, is focusing on the uniquely feminine but not limiting the possibility of female contributions to society. In fact, his conclusions are much the same as ones that Gilligan (1982) was to come to later. Speaking of identity in women, Erikson says, "Granted that something in the young woman's identity must keep itself open for the peculiarities of the man to be joined and of the children to be brought up, I think that much of a young woman's identity is already defined in her kind of attractiveness and in the selective nature of her search for the man (or men) by whom she wishes to be sought. . . . This, of course, is only the psychosexual aspect of her identity, and she may go far in postponing its closure while training herself as a worker and a citizen and while developing as a person within the role possibilities of her time" (1968, p. 283). Later he comes as close as he ever does to defining identity in women: "Womanhood arrives when attractiveness and experience have succeeded in selecting what is to be admitted to the welcome of the inner space 'for keeps' " (p. 283).

Models of Development

Psychologists who wish to shape a theory to describe female development have been at a loss because of the absence of a comprehensive paradigm on which to build. Classical psychoanalytic theory is grounded in the genital inferiority of women and deduces their moral inferiority as well. New appreciation of the importance to women of preoedipal aspects of development has replaced the classical psychoanalytic focus on the oedipal stage of development (Eichenbaum and Orbach, 1983).

Object-relations theory has seemed a promising avenue within psychoanalysis for grounding an understanding of women's development. Fairbairn (1952) and Winnicott (1958, 1965) radically revised Freud's central idea that objects (other people) are necessary for drive gratification, that drive propels social life. The assumption of the object-relations school is that human need for other humans is independent of drive, that humans are born object seeking. Issues of relatedness—among them separation-individuation—replace libido as organizing aspects of ego development. Basic conflicts are about the complexities of loving rather than sexual fulfillment. Self-definition and object relations are inextricably linked.

Development itself, in traditional male terms, is seen as a movement from dependence to autonomy, as the unfolding of a chrysalis with the end result an independent hero who stands alone and pursues his achievements. The major studies of male development during adulthood (Vaillant, 1977; Levinson and others, 1978) have found career, achievement, and independence to be organizing principles of identity in men. Relationships with others are secondary to these men; their life course rotates on an axis of being and becoming in relation to career goals. The lives of these men present coherent, fairly linear trajectories as they progress or fall behind on their paths.

Developmental psychologists and clinicians have commented on the inadequacy of existing developmental models to illuminate women's lives (Rossi, 1980; Unger, 1983; Lerman, 1986; Peck, 1986). In addition to calling for a theory that will include the importance of relatedness and attachment in women's lives, these writers have stressed the need for a theory flexible enough to encompass the multiplicity of roles and circumstances in women's lives. Neither a fixed-stage model, such as Levinson devised for men, nor a timing-of-events model (Neugarten and Datan, 1973) will adequately describe the complexity of women's life circumstances.

There has not yet been a longitudinal study of women, but we now know enough about women to be able to phrase some meaningful questions. This book is an effort to view identity in women in women's own terms. It leaves open the possibility that both achievement and interpersonal aspects of life are important. It is an effort to understand the ways in which women consolidate identity and to look at the differences among them.

Chapter 3

Four Pathways
to Identity

> "Identity" and "identity crisis" have in popular and scientific usage become terms which alternately circumscribe something so large and so seemingly self-evident that to demand a definition would seem petty, while at other times they designate something made so narrow for purposes of measurement that the overall meaning is lost, and it could just as well be called something else.
>
> —*Erik Erikson, Identity, Youth and Crisis*

Erikson deliberately left his concept of ego identity connotative and descriptive in order to allow for the multiple levels of meaning he attempted to articulate. How then can those who wish to study identity make objective something that is only a vaguely experienced subjective phenomenon? If identity is the fabric, looking at the individual strands will tell us little. As Erikson says, if we do this, we are then looking at something else. Identity, as a concept, is an emergent phenomenon, greater than the sum of the parts. This enigma posed a great problem for psychological researchers, accustomed as they are to dissecting phenomena, who wished to understand differences among adolescents in their approach to the identity-formation task.

Identity is not quantifiable. One cannot have a lot of identity or a little bit of it, although one can be without a sense of identity. Because identity is a configuration of aspects of personality, we must think of qualitative differences among identities, of differences in the ways they are formulated, but we must preserve the holistic nature of identity.

The Research Paradigm

Although a number of investigators (see Bourne, 1978a, 1978b, for a complete review) have made efforts to operationalize Erikson's concept of ego identity, the most widely used approach has followed a methodology developed by Marcia (1966) that preserves the integrity of Erikson's formulation. Marcia approached the study of identity formation as a dynamic process. He made Erikson's theory of identity formation researchable by focusing on crisis and commitment to identity elements. Following Erikson's theory, Marcia reasoned that to forge an identity, the individual must experience some crisis in ideas derived from the ascribed identity of childhood. The young person must consider options of occupation and ideology. Then, having weighed possibilities, perhaps experimented with different choices, the young person, at the end of adolescence, must make commitments about what to become and what to believe. These commitments become the core of this newly wrought identity. Those who successfully transcend crisis and make such commitments can be assumed to have achieved, at least, a stage-specific identity. Those who avoid the process, neither experiencing crisis in identity matters nor forming commitments, are in states of identity *diffusion.*

But, Marcia reasoned, there are two intermediate possibilities as well. A young person may bypass the identity stage altogether by merely carrying forward previously incorporated, parentally derived standards and goals. Such people might be considered to have *foreclosed* identities. Or, a young person might be in the midst of a *moratorium* phase, still questing, trying to resolve identity-related questions and make commitments.

Marcia defined four types (statuses) of identity formation based on the presence or absence of crisis and commitment in occupational and ideological (religious and political) realms. This

typology of developmental progression can be assessed objec-
tively.

The first type is Identity Foreclosure. These young people have made commitments in the absence of a searching or
crisis phase. They have carried forward either parentally derived
expectations or childhood plans and beliefs without subjecting
them to question or scrutiny. Their identity formation is premature, rooted in earlier (preadolescent) phases of development.

The second type is Identity Achievement, which describes
young people who have undergone the process of testing options, then committing themselves to ways of being.

The third type of identity formation is Moratorium.
These people are actively in a crisis or exploratory phase. They
are struggling to make commitments but have not yet found the
right ones for them.

In the fourth type, Identity Diffusion, young people are
experiencing neither crisis nor commitment. They have abandoned childhood resolutions but are not struggling for new
ones. They are drifting, avoiding the identity-formation task.

The labels for the groups are, to be sure, a bit jarring and,
in some cases, mildly pejorative. But they have been used for
research since 1966, and to change them now would only induce confusion. Marcia (1980) emphasizes that there are both
healthy and pathological aspects to each of the styles: Foreclosures (from foreclosing possibility) can be viewed as either
loyal or rigid, cooperative or conforming; Moratoriums (after
Erikson's nomenclature for the period of identity testing) may
be judged either flexible or indecisive, philosophical or anxious;
Diffusions (also after Erikson's terminology) can be seen to be
either carefree or irresponsible, creative or disaffected. The
Identity Achievements are, perhaps, the most poorly named,
for identity is never an achievement. To call them the commit-
ment-through-crisis group is, however, too cumbersome. Although they are largely seen to be independent and self-directed
there is also room for concern about whether they remain flexible enough, whether their commitments are premature. The
labels, then, are meant to be descriptive rather than evaluative.

In Marcia's formulation, following Erikson's theory, adolescents are presumed to begin the identity-formation period as either Foreclosures or Diffusions, either rooted in a childhood identity or without a sense of coherence and purpose. The height of the identity-crisis stage occurs, at least among college students, from ages eighteen to twenty-two, when they are granted a Moratorium period to explore, test, and rework identity possibilities. Out of this period of seeking and grappling should grow the personal investments that are the core of Identity Achievement.

Not all young people, however, follow this path toward successful resolution of identity issues. Some become mired in perpetual indecision (Moratoriums); others eschew possibility in favor of unreflective choice (Foreclosures); still others permit themselves to be carried along by external forces (Diffusions). Defining these four groups allows for exploration of the differences among young people who follow one path or the other.

Using an extensive interview, Marcia and his co-workers found that they could divide college students into these four identity categories (or statuses) with remarkable reliability. The differences among the groups were differences in development or personality style; there were no differences in intelligence (Marcia, 1966, 1976; Marcia and Friedman, 1970; Schenkel, 1975).*

This research paradigm, known as *identity-status research*, has become the dominant one for research in identity formation (Bourne, 1978a, 1978b). Consistent findings from research using this paradigm have helped to explicate the adolescent process. (See Bourne, 1978a, 1978b, Marcia, 1980, and Waterman, 1982, for complete reviews.) Those in the Moratorium group, for example, were found as expected to be the most anxious, while Foreclosures were the least anxious. Identity Achievements and Moratoriums were found to have the

---

*Construct validation was demonstrated by the capacity of the identity-status categories to discriminate young people in a theoretically consistent manner on such variables as goal setting, authoritarianism, and vulnerability to self-esteem manipulation (Marcia, 1966).

highest self-esteem (Marcia, 1976; Marcia and Friedman, 1970), to be less impulsive (Waterman and Waterman, 1974) and more culturally sophisticated (Waterman and Waterman, 1971).

Research along these lines was fruitful until someone tried to produce the same results with women as subjects. Then, as with so much research derived from men and then applied to women, the consistency and predictability of findings broke down (Schenkel and Marcia, 1972).

Marcia had been using Erikson's dimensions of occupation and ideology, the latter subdivided into religious and political ideology, as the arenas in which crisis and commitment were assessed. Not until Schenkel added a fourth category, that of sexual values and standards, could women be meaningfully divided into the same four groups, with the same reliability and predictive validity as had been obtained with the short interview in an all-male sample (Schenkel and Marcia, 1972). Schenkel's research showed that, for women, identity decisions regarding religion and sexual values were more predictive of overall identity status than were decisions regarding occupation or political ideology.

With this addition to the identity-status assessment, identity status among women could now be reliably determined. But then another puzzling finding appeared. Whereas for men the theoretically "high" statuses, Identity Achievement and Moratorium, were repeatedly found to consist of the healthier, developmentally more mature subjects, a different pattern appeared for women. Among female subjects, the committed groups—the Identity Achievements and Foreclosures—scored highest on psychologically valued dimensions such as self-esteem, low anxiety, and field independence (Marcia and Friedman, 1970; Schenkel and Marcia, 1972; Toder and Marcia, 1973; Prager, 1982). In other words, Foreclosure was an "undesirable" status for men but was associated with desirable characteristics among women. And whereas Moratorium was a "healthy" or "high" status for males, it was "low" and associated with unfavorable variables among women. This finding raised the sobering question of whether our society somehow discouraged exploration of identity possibilities for women.

Perhaps women were being differentially rewarded for making identity commitments, however premature (Marcia and Friedman, 1970; Schenkel, 1975; Orlofsky, 1978; Marcia, 1980; Prager, 1982).

That the Moratorium phase seemed to be such an unsettling one for women during their late adolescence was a troubling finding and a difficult one to understand. Surely these women would resolve their identity questions eventually and ultimately show the ego strength typical of male Moratoriums. By the same token, the Foreclosure position seemed to be an untenable one, sure to catch up with these young women as they grew into adulthood (Ginsburg and Orlofsky, 1981; Josselson, 1982).

The Present Study

My work in this field began with an effort, in 1971, to understand the internal and developmental roots of identity formation in women. I wanted to explore the internal differences among the four groups of women that would explain why some resolve identity crises and integrate identities while others either avoid the task of creating an identity or become unable to transcend crisis.

Over a period of three years, I intensively interviewed sixty female college students, chosen randomly from college lists, at four quite different colleges and universities. I summed up my findings by drawing brief portraits of each of the identity statuses (Josselson, 1973).

My work showed that women in the four identity-status groups differed consistently, reflecting different modes of negotiating the challenges of adolescence. These women approached the identity-formation task with the selves they brought to their adolescence. The Identity Achievements were women who could rework their childhood selves in a comfortable, tolerable way, defining a path for themselves that they felt they had truly chosen. The Moratoriums, by contrast, were leaving home, sometimes dramatically and always guiltily, in search of a feeling of absolute rightness that eluded them. Life appeared most complicated to the Moratoriums. Emotionally sensitive and reflective, they experienced so much conflict about what to be, whom to believe, and how to behave that they remained unable to choose a path for themselves.

The Foreclosures were women who could not psychologically leave home at all. Preoccupied with security, which was founded in an intense and early attachment to one or the other parent, they were unable to relinquish the gratifications of love and care that independent selfhood would require. Rigid and moralistic, though hardworking and high achieving, they remained securely embedded in their family network and bypassed exploration of identity. Those who were Diffuse in identity showed a range of pathological problems and early developmental conflicts that made it impossible to work on identity-formation tasks. They brought to their adolescence too few inner psychological resources to address identity decisions seriously.

After ten years of presenting my findings to various groups, I became haunted by the idea that these women, frozen in print, were out there living their lives. I wanted to know what became of them. And I wanted to know whether my predictions about them were accurate. Did identity status in college make an important difference in the life course each group was following? Did the Moratoriums reach identity resolutions and go on to become Identity Achievements? Did the Foreclosures have difficulties as a result of the rigidity and lack of personality differentiation that they showed as late adolescents? Did the Identity Achievements maintain their commitments, or did they again undergo crisis periods? And what became of the often-troubled Diffusions? I hoped that answers to these questions would also shed some light on the dominant issues of women's development and bring into relief the different pathways that women follow along the road of identity.

To conduct the original study, names were drawn randomly from lists of senior women at four colleges and universities. Only students aged twenty to twenty-two were included. These students were contacted by letter and follow-up phone call and invited to participate in the study. A total of sixty women were interviewed intensively. Data were gathered by clinical psychologists; each subject was interviewed for two to three hours. Taped interviews were then transcribed and analyzed. (See Appendix A for a full description of the methodology.)

For the follow-up study, thirty-four women could be located and agreed to participate. They were sent a lengthy questionnaire and tapes on which to record their responses to open-ended questions. After the tapes were transcribed, my research assistants and I recontacted the women for telephone or personal interviews to clarify and deepen the data until we felt that we understood the important aspects of each woman's life. Most interviews lasted three to four hours.

At the time of the first, college-age, interview, each woman responded to the questions of the Identity-Status Interview (see Appendix B), which allowed the researchers to assign her to one of the four identity statuses. Assignment was made, as described earlier, by assessment of her level of crisis and commitment in each of four areas: occupation, religion, politics, and sexual values and standards. The identity status in which a woman best fit in college is considered to be her assignment group for the comparison purposes of this follow-up study.

All names have been changed and identifying data disguised in order to preserve the privacy of each individual. But because identifying information is the very stuff of identity, I have tried to make the disguise as close in spirit to the truth as possible.

The Women of the Study

The women to be discussed in this book are, in many ways, ordinary women. They were not chosen because of some special achievement, nor were they drawn from the top universities. However, they are not women who came to our attention by virtue of being deviant—that is, patients or political gadflies. They are "normal" women who happened to be seniors in average colleges and who were chosen at random and asked to share their lives with me. There were no statistically significant differences among the identity statuses on any of the social or cognitive variables that might be of concern—that is, there were no differences in social class or intelligence among the four identity-status groups. Therefore, before looking at the four groups individually, it makes sense to set the stage by describing these women as a large group overall.

Although they were of high enough intelligence and aspiration to be in college at that time, these women were drawn from all social strata. Some were from farm backgrounds; others came from the privileged sector of society. Half of them had fathers who were college graduates, but only 17 percent had mothers who attended college. Most were the first generation of women in their families to attend college—a source of pride for them as well as their families, representing as it did the attainment of their parents' ambitions for them and the possibility of upward social mobility.

Although parents often pressured their daughters to attend college, they seldom steered them in a particular occupational direction. Most of the women, as college seniors, reported that although their parents were happy with their occupational plans, they were more interested in having them marry than succeed professionally. Their parents seem to have viewed their daughters' college education as a means of self-improvement or husband catching.

Many of these women, as college seniors, were involved in long-standing relationships with men, and several were engaged or recently married. Most, however, felt no immediate press to marry, although nearly all intended to marry "eventually." As a group they held few romantic ideas about marriage. Rather, they saw marriage as satisfying their needs for long-term companionship and perhaps for raising a family. The majority of these women, however, said that they wished to be on their own for a while, even though their graduation without marriage prospects was, in many cases, a source of friction with their parents.

Asked about plans for having children, these women, at age twenty-one, almost unanimously replied, "That's so far off." All but two planned to have children "eventually." As they envisioned their lives from the threshold of college graduation, the most common plan was a sequence of a few years of nonmarriage and career involvement, several years of childless marriage in which both partners work, several years of child-rearing and not working, followed by a return to some sort of involvement in a career, a part-time job, or volunteer efforts. No woman in the sample envisioned herself living a life of full-time homemaking and mothering.

This group's college majors were diverse. Although several planned to go to graduate school, most did not. Most were in service-oriented fields and had high ideals for what they hoped to give to others. Most had identified some group—children, the medically ill, the disadvantaged—who they felt needed their help. These women worried that they might not be able to accomplish enough in helping them.

At the time of the first interview, the women were looking forward to college graduation, to having their first "real" jobs, and to financial autonomy. After years of working part-time and scrimping to get through school, their first full-time job meant their own apartments or cars or clothes or travel, and these attractions were central in their minds as they approached graduation.

Coming of age in the early seventies, they were all exposed to feminist ideology, but foremost in their imaginations were private hopes: for love and family, for good jobs and material comfort. Most were apolitical, even during the ferment of the late 1960s and early 1970s, when they were in college. In fact, I was often amazed that so many of these women were unable to think of any contemporary political question on which they had any views at all. Some did take part in anti-Vietnam War protests or the student strikes that took place on some campuses. Some women had become concerned about the Equal Rights Amendment, an important political issue of the time.

Many of these women were deeply religious. Among the sample were Catholics, Protestants, and Jews, and some who had no religious affiliation at all. For most, during adolescence, the question of the existence of God had been a major and important one to be puzzled about and wrestled with and resolved.

In sexual standards and values, there was a good deal of

difference among these women. Although "Make love not war" was the slogan of their generation, one-quarter of the sample were virgins at the time of the college interview, while less than one-eighth had experimented with free, nondiscriminating sexuality. The majority viewed sex as a concomitant of love, an expression of love to be treated with respect and engaged in with careful discrimination and proven emotion in regard to partners. Nearly all these women, however, regarded their parents as prohibiting their sexuality. Some talked of how their mothers would have heart attacks if they were to discover their daughters' sexual behavior. The women who were sexually active in college saw themselves as doing something forbidden.

Nearly all these women came from intact families where the father worked and the mother did not, at least while the children were growing up. Many of these women worked to pay their college tuition and learned responsibility early.

Interviewed as college seniors, these women spoke vividly and expressively about the aspects of their lives they were most invested in. Left to define what was most important to them, they focused on the most immediate aspects of their lives— papers, exams, boyfriends, girlfriends, money. Their identities, if one may think of a composite identity, were unimaginative and conventional. They were loath to see themselves as part of history, feeling in general that they as individuals were too insignificant to affect the lives of any but a few chosen others. They were also willing to choose among ordinary social alternatives rather than to create new ones, even though the times made inventive choices appear quite realistic. This was the generation that was supposed to be dropping out, turning on, and tuning in. They were to remake the world, reject materialism and imperialism, and not trust anyone over thirty. At least those were the slogans and battle cries. If, for any generation in recent history, anything seemed to be possible, it was theirs. Only a few years older than my subjects, I had been involved in the dominant ideology of this generation. Therefore, I was somewhat surprised to discover such conventionality among the women in this group.

Most could not imagine their lives five years later, even

with respect to a geographical locale. Their identities, therefore, had a kind of built-in flexibility. They were prepared for what might come. Their ideologies were interpersonal: They knew what kind of person they wanted to be—open, honest, caring. How they would express this identity awaited the circumstances that would unfold.

When reinterviewed ten to twelve years later (1982-1984) these women had diverged widely and were far less homogeneous cohorts than they had been in college. Then, they were students living in two large cities. Now, they live in fourteen different states and one foreign country. Most live in small towns or suburbs of a large city. Few are living the urban life popularized by the media.

By occupation, they include a lawyer, a judge, a doctor, a psychologist, physical therapists, nurses, teachers, social workers, writers, businesswomen, and full-time homemakers. In general, they are far less idealistic about their occupational goals than they were in college. Reality has caught up with them, and they all express some disillusionment with the world of work. Those who had high hopes for effecting social change have come up against the reluctance of society to change. Others who hoped to help just a few have found out how few could be helped. Nearly all who work in institutions or large organizations mention dissatisfaction with bureaucracy that seems to impede their work.

Their personal lives have also diverged. Some have decided not to have children; some have already had two or three. There are single, married, divorced, and remarried women. Some married right after college as planned; others have married for the first time in the past two or three years.

As in college, these women continue to be rather apolitical. If they mention a political concern, it tends to be a local issue that directly affects them, usually through their children. Some who had been active during the antiwar protests of the Viet Nam era speak of having become disillusioned with the political process and turning their back on it. Only two of these women identify themselves as feminists or belong to feminist organizations. If the others mention feminist issues, it tends to be in connection with personal instances of job discrimination or hopes that their children will grow up without sexist ideas of what is possible for men and women.

As a group, they are slightly less religious than they were in college. One-third of them have a deep religious commitment that is a central aspect of their lives; one-half have no religious affiliation at all.

One-third of the women have had some contact with psychotherapy at some point during the last fifteen years. Generally their therapeutic experiences were for brief periods, for help with some problem about a relationship. Some sought marriage counseling; others sought support after the break-up of a relationship. Several have had extended psychotherapy for long-standing personality difficulties such as depression, but these are the minority.

To those accustomed to reading the clinical literature, these women will seem unfamiliar and, perhaps, superficial. The discourse of psychological health and adequate adjustment is quite different from what we are accustomed to hearing in our consulting rooms. These are women who tend not to magnify discontent or to focus on difficulties. Problems are seen as roadblocks to be overcome as quickly as possible in order to return to a smoothly running life. These women tend not to be deeply insightful or interested in self-knowledge. Overall, they judge themselves by how others around them, who are like them, are doing. As a group, they are reasonably satisfied with their lives. They consider themselves happy.

To those accustomed to reading the popular literature, these women may also seem surprising. They are not immersed in the conflicts so endemic to the media woman. Those who want careers and families have found ways of doing so and feel relatively little conflict about it. They are not interested in social change.

What does interest these women, besides the people they love, are their leisure pursuits. Most of them exercise regularly and engage in a variety of sports. Many have hobbies that occupy them, such as needlepoint or cooking or gardening. Most of them are fiercely interested in the places where they live and enjoy tending and decorating their houses or apartments. All seem to be in a developmental stage of material acquisition, and economic concerns are often paramount in their decision making. Most, especially the mothers who also work outside the home, say that their biggest problem is not having enough time to do everything and no time at all for themselves.

Although several of these women have become well known locally through their professions, the group as a whole is not a distinguished one. Rather, they are a group that can be viewed as typical or average, at least for college-educated women. (It will remain for future researchers to investigate identity among a non-college-educated sample.) A sample as small as this cannot be considered representative of all women. But they do represent a group of women who are not studied, reported about, or understood often. Because they are engaged mainly in living quiet lives, they rarely come to our attention. They would not have volunteered for a study such as this one when they were in college, but they were curious, and I paid them at a time when they could use the few dollars. For the current interviews, I prevailed on them, begged and cajoled, reminded them that they had participated before and were therefore irreplaceable. Some were hesitant at the beginning of the interviews, then seemed to welcome the opportunity to reflect on their lives with an interested listener. They spoke openly and articulately about their lives, their thoughts and feelings, and some commented perceptively on the particularly intense kind of discussion that is sometimes possible only with an interested and uncritical stranger. Both in college and as adults, I found them delightful to interview. Each has a unique story to tell. In her own way, each has had a share of joy and pain.

Chapter 4

 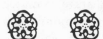

Purveyors of
the Heritage:
The Foreclosures

Each Morn a thousand Roses brings, you say;
Yes, but where leaves the Rose of Yesterday?
—*Edward FitzGerald,*
The Rubáiyát of Omar Khayyám

Fern and Felicia are living out their childhood dreams. From an early age, they had a picture of how they wanted their lives to unfold, and they have pursued their goals with single-minded determination. They illustrate the group of women classified as Foreclosures, women who, at the end of college, had made identity commitments without undergoing a period of crisis. Their choices of goals and values rested largely on assumptions or identifications based in childhood; they had carried these choices forward without doubt or hesitation.

A typical Foreclosure response to occupational decisions, for example, was to say that she had wanted to be a teacher since she was in grade school or that she had chosen law because her father thought it would be good for her. Similarly, with regard to religion, Foreclosures were likely to continue in the beliefs and practices of their childhoods, without rethinking or questioning. Most blindly adopted their parents' standards with regard to sexual morality and were likely to say that they did so because they had been raised with those standards or because they could not risk disappointing their parents.

In other research, the Foreclosure group has presented a continuing enigma. Whereas for men the Foreclosure status is considered and has been empirically determined to be "low" in ego identity and therefore a maladaptive form of identity resolution, the opposite appears to be true for women. In general, Foreclosure women behave on objective measures much like Achievement women. They show the same tough-mindedness and ability to resist pressure to conform, the same high self-esteem, and even lower anxiety than the Identity Achievements (Marcia and Friedman, 1970). Some writers have wondered whether, because our culture demands less autonomy from women, autonomy is rewarded less in women (Schenkel, 1975; Prager, 1982). If that were so, then the relative dependence of the Foreclosures would not cause them difficulty in society or be related to maladjustment. It has remained unclear whether the Foreclosures' rigidity and lack of personality growth at adolescence put them at risk for psychological disturbance later on.

The follow-up data demonstrate that these women continue to live out the identity decisions they formulated long ago. They demonstrate a style of being a woman in today's world, a style based on tradition and conviction, rooted in psychological needs for security and constancy. They continue to adapt well to their lives, to maintain their self-esteem and their strength. They settle into life with firm ideas of how they want their lives to go and never waver in their resolution.

Fern

Fern in College. When interviewed as a senior in college, Fern was attending a large state university, majoring in nursing. She had never doubted any of her strong Catholic religious beliefs and categorically felt that premarital intercourse was wrong because she had been taught so in school. She had no time for political thinking and trusted "the men who guide the country" to make wise decisions. In the four areas of decision making

that define the identity statuses, then, Fern was clearly Foreclosed. She had never experienced a period of exploration or
testing but was firmly committed to a life plan.

From her earliest years, Fern felt great sympathy toward
those less fortunate than herself. Her father had a slowly metas-
tasizing cancer and was ill from the time she was old enough to
remember. A significant memory from her early childhood concerned a crippled child who lived next door. None of the neighborhood children would play with this child, but Fern felt com-
passion for her and spent hours entertaining her rather than
joining in the games of the other children. This activity seemed
to parallel those of Fern's mother, who devoted much of her
energy to caring for Fern's father. With the helping pattern
firmly entrenched in her family, Fern felt born to be a nurse.

Raised and still living in an Irish Catholic section of Boston, Fern emphasized the extraordinary closeness of her family.
She, her mother, and her brother were all centered on caring for
her father until he died when Fern was eleven. The financial
burdens caused by his death only increased their closeness. "Because he was sick, we could never go far from home. I had a lot
of chores, a lot of responsibilities after he died. A lot of my
views became very adult. I was different from the kids at school,
and I had no time for going along with the crowd."

A strong religious faith kept Fern uplifted and hopeful
throughout her life. But religion was also a source of conflict.
Fern's father was not Catholic, and the family feared that if he
did not convert, they would lose him forever after his death,
with all hope of a heavenly reunion shattered. Nightly, Fern and
her mother prayed for his recovery from his illness—and for his
conversion. Fern's Catholic schooling reinforced her religious
focus, and for a long time, as a child, she dreamed of becoming
a nun.

Fern described her father as having been friendly and out-
going, always warm and available to listen to his children's problems and worries. Her mother was more introverted and had no
friends outside the family. Fern saw her parents in an idealized
way. With deep feeling, she said, "I don't think I could pick parents who have given more to their children than my parents did

to me." There was never argument in the family. Family councils were convened to resolve disputes about chores and money. Of herself, Fern gave the impression of having been a model child, eager to please her parents and convinced of their ultimate wisdom.

It was difficult, during this interview, to prod Fern to talk of her life and experience outside of religion and family. To almost all questions, she responded with reference to her family, their beliefs and goals for her. They wanted her to be the best she could be, to work hard, to have high ideals. When stressed or saddened, Fern turned to her patron saint to ask for help or guidance and, in times of great frustration, went to church to speak directly to God.

Life outside the family was fraught with difficulty. In her first friendship with a neighborhood playmate at age eight, Fern was rejected because her Protestant chum's mother did not want her daughter playing with a Catholic. She remembers returning home to her mother in tears and of "becoming aware of what kinds of things exist." Her mother consoled her, telling her that she was right, that there were mean people in the world and you could only, in the end, trust your own family. Her mother never pushed her out into the neighborhood, never nagged her to invite friends home. Fern retreated to the safety and security of the warm, close-knit family. Even in college, Fern said, "I have many acquaintances, but few friends." Her strict moral code made it difficult for her to join in pleasurable activities with others. She could not understand, for example, why her classmates drank or smoked pot; she could "get high on life." Similarly, she shut off a budding friendship with a girl in one of her classes when this girl began cutting class. Fern tended to form friendships, or acquaintanceships, by nurturing others, listening to their problems, doing things for them, helping them through difficulties. Sometimes she sought support from them. But she was wary with friends, sensitive to rejection and easily slighted.

The college experience had little impact on Fern beyond her success in her nurse's training course. She found the teachers to be impersonal, not interested in her, and classmates to be absorbed in their own pursuits. She spent her free time, when she was not working or in class, playing with young children in her neighborhood or taking care of someone in her church who needed looking after.

The death of her father was a major traumatic event for Fern and left her in search of an idealized male substitute. In high school, the most important person in her life became an English teacher who rescued her from her isolation and withdrawal and got her involved in producing plays. "If it weren't for him, I'd probably be a very dull person," she said. "He helped me gain confidence and learn to relate to other people."

Relationships with men her own age were more problematic. She had dated little, and the one brief relationship she formed ended when the man was unable to tolerate her criticism of him. She was doubtful about her femininity throughout college and worried about being a spinster. Sex was something of a mystery to her. She thought it was probably necessary, even before marriage, but she thought she would be disappointed in herself if she did it. Probably, she thought, if she were going to have sex, she would ask her mother to get her birth-control pills, but her mother firmly believed that if you have sex before marriage, the man will just "dump you." Although she feared remaining unmarried, Fern said that she could not compromise her standards for a man and could not love a man who did not respect her scruples. "I'm not willing to change. Someone will have to like me as I am—respect my standards and beliefs."

As Fern looked toward the future, she very much wanted marriage and children. But she expected to continue to work, at least part-time. Through acid experience, she had learned the perils of being unskilled as a woman, having to work at menial jobs as her mother did to support a family. She wanted to be sure of having a profession to fall back on and, even more, she did not want to waste the helping skills that would benefit others.

At a deep level, Fern wanted to be a saint. In the interview, she tried to present herself as quasi-perfect and, in her life, tried to live out this ideal. Some of this quest was tied to an unconscious effort to be worthy of her idealized father, who died before she could internally separate from him. One of her dreams evinced this unconscious theme. "I dreamt I met B [the boyfriend] again, and I was very cool to him. I told him I was going for a walk, and he came along. We walked to the beach, and we began to talk about what had happened, and he was just about to tell me what he felt, and then I woke up. So I'll never know what he would have said." This dream symbolically expresses what Fern feels happened with her father. But "what he would have said" was firmly a part of her, and it was toward these ideals that Fern organized her life.

Fear of loss of control was a central dynamic in her unconscious life. Her voice was confident and her manner relaxed (although she was eager to convince me of her goodness), but the unconscious material belied a massive fear of helplessness and intense needs for defense against it. Here is a recurrent dream Fern reported at that time: "People are running back and forth in chaos, yelling and screaming. I am standing in the middle, and I don't know what's going on. I'm watching all these people running around, and I don't know why I'm standing there instead of running with everyone else. And I don't know where anyone's going or why they're so frightened, and I want to get out."

In this pained and terrifying dream is the chaos Fern experienced from her impulses. The frantic melee is very much the dark underside of the neat, ordered, careful existence Fern maintained in her waking life. The dream represents some of Fern's experience of the nonfamilial world, a world she could not understand or find a niche in. And "getting out" for her, throughout her life, had been retreat to the security and safety of her family, her religion, and the ideals she derived from them. The rethinking and loosening of control that the process of identity formation entails would have overwhelmed her. Safety and control, organization, planning, and goodness were most important. Giving to others was a way of escaping the frightening inner contradictions of the self.

At the end of college, Fern had made clear identity commitments. Her choice of nursing as a profession and her clear re-

ligious and moral values linked her to the world and also helped
her deal with conscious and unconscious personality conflicts.
The history of Fern's relationship with her father left her with
strong ideals about helping others as well as deep conflicts
about relationships with men.

In many ways, Fern, at the end of college, was a proto-
typic Foreclosure. She made it easy to understand the basis for
the research findings of positive personality attributes among
Foreclosures. Cemented into a system of values, rooted in dependency on family, Fern was sure of herself, unanxious, able
to resist peer pressure, and she had high self-esteem. Yet, over
the years, when I presented this case at various professional con-
ferences, people were quick to point out all the neuroticism in
Fern: She overuses repression, remains psychologically a little
girl, has poor interpersonal relationships, has not resolved her
relationship to her father. Others would point out the possible
paranoia in her mother, the underlying depression Fern is only
barely containing, the hidden rage Fern must feel at not having
been given all that much by her parents. Psychologists were
unanimous in predicting a poor outcome for Fern. This is not
identity, they said of her career goals, this is symptom formation.

The follow-up data add information but do not resolve
the question of whether Fern is neurotic or not. She has continued to be much like she was in college, without symptoms or
depression. She appears to have made her identity resolution
work.

Fern at Thirty-Three. Fern realized her lifelong dream of
serving others by becoming a nurse as she planned. Moving up
through the ranks, she became the head nurse of a children's
ward in a large hospital. Her job carries great responsibility,
both for patients and staff.

Now age thirty-three, Fern remains deeply involved in her
Catholic faith. In times of distress, she prays, and she often feels
that her petitions through prayer are answered. She observes all
church rituals, including regular attendance at Mass. She married a man who was not Catholic, secretly hoping that she could

persuade him to convert, thus repeating with her husband her mother's experience with her father. Only after several years was she able to succeed, and they then renewed their wedding vows as Catholics. She and her husband now give confirmation classes and teach marriage preparation under the auspices of the Church.

Fern is involved in community issues and local politics. She is particularly dedicated to matters pertaining to education and worked loyally for a candidate who supported her views.

Fern's views on sex have not changed from her late-adolescent values. She continues to believe that premarital sex encourages relationships without long-lasting commitment, which she finds unacceptable.

Twelve years later, then, Fern is much the same as she was in college, despite the outward changes in her life. She negotiated the developmental tasks of early adulthood by finding people and situations that were consonant with her sense of identity or by coercing them to conform to her.

Fern met Roger just after her graduation from college. She found his goals and values to be compatible with hers; they loved each other; and they married a year later. Roger works as a respiratory therapist and was supportive of Fern's occupational goals. Their marriage was based on achieving mutual goals and proceeded smoothly until Fern feared that she might be unable to convince him to convert to Catholicism. At this point, she turned to her priest for support, and, at the time of the birth of their first child, Roger finally agreed.

Fern feels that Roger is somewhat of a fun-loving person, and they clash over her strong moral stance about some of his activities. He enjoys playing poker, for example, which Fern finds nearly intolerable. The source of her greatest disappointment in him, however, is that she feels he is not as giving or as affectionate as she is. But she appreciates his support of her career goals, his willingness to allow her time for volunteer activities. The most important part of their relationship is that they know that they "always have each other." Fern reports having made a good sexual adjustment. They enjoy their sexual life together, although they have sex infrequently. Roger makes her

feel accepted and loved for who she is, and she considers herself
to be happily married.

The affection that she feels Roger denies her she tends to
derive from her two children. She describes her daughters, now
aged five and two, as "an extension of my life." She had always
wanted children, and they waited until Roger finished his training to try to conceive. When conception did not occur right
away, Fern was frustrated by the failure of biology to cooperate
with her carefully planned life. It took a full year of waiting before she became pregnant. From reading advice in childrearing
books, Fern decided that spacing children three years apart was
optimal, and this time biology cooperated. She especially enjoyed her children's infancy, when they needed her most and
made so many changes. She had difficulty mothering them
when they were at what she termed the "defiant" stage. All of
the doting she had wanted to lavish on Roger she now gives to
her daughters. Fern and Roger had decided not to have any
more children, but, in the past year, Fern became aware of a
strong wish for a son as well as a wish to have an infant again.
They have therefore decided to try to conceive again.

Fern does most of the childrearing, all the house clean-
ing, works full-time, and has a number of volunteer charitable
projects. It is striking that she has no expectation that her husband contribute more labor to the household, nor does she have
any doubts that she could handle responsibility for another
child. She has had moments of intense guilt about not always
being there when her children may have needed her but does
not doubt the rightness of her decision to work.

Financially, Fern and Roger have had to struggle to make
ends meet. They are proud of owning their own home, but
there is little money left over for entertainment, travel, or fun.
When they do have extra money, they spend it on treats for the
children.

With all the activity and stress in her life, Fern continues
to have excellent health. She has rarely missed a day of work,
does not smoke, drink, or take drugs. She copes with stress
through prayer and through it she decides that everything happens for a purpose, even if we do not know what it is.

In her current life, Fern has realized her dream of estab-
lishing a complete family unit to compensate for the one she
was deprived of in childhood. Although she says that she is disillusioned that her marriage is not the perfect one that she had
dreamed of, she feels that she has learned that "this is what life
is" and gratifies her unmet needs through her children and her
work.

Fern has maintained her close relationship to her mother, who stays with Fern's family for four months each year. Her
mother has been depressed since her retirement, and Fern feels
that she now has the opportunity to repay her mother for supporting her through her rough times. Although her mother is a
help with the children, Fern emphasizes that her main interest
in these visits is to support and encourage her mother. She feels
that they share even more now than they did when she was in
college.

Looking back and reflecting on her life from age thirty-
three, Fern sees herself as having been a shy, lonely child who
managed to make herself outstanding to adults but was unable
to cope with her peers. The illness and death of her father still
loom as the critical events in her life. Her gratitude toward
the teacher who "brought her out of her cocoon" remains a
central part of her autobiography. From this vantage point,
Fern considers her college education to have been an important
force in freeing her from her sense of insecurity and inferiority.
Since college, Fern had two important professional mentors,
both men, who challenged her abilities and helped her refine
and upgrade her skills as a nurse.

Although she had been looking forward to being on her
own after college, Fern deeply felt the need for someone to
share her life with. Despite her disillusionment and disappointments in her marriage, Fern describes her life now as one of
contentment and fulfillment. She feels that she has grown in
that she no longer pursues the unattainable but still "always
reaches for a little bit more."

Looking back on her experiences in college, Fern regrets
having limited her involvement to skill development. She wishes
she had participated more in college activities, had had more

friends, and had prepared herself more for the world. She continues to have few friends, as her life is bounded by family and work.

When she looks to the future, Fern's hope is to be able to continue to provide for others. She hopes to continue her contributions to her field, to help other professionals develop their skills, and to be part of the growth of her department. Her wish for her family is that she be able to continue to live with all of them (clearly a wish that she not repeat her father's life) and "to provide for my children all things, material and nonmaterial, to make them loving, caring human beings."

In Fern, we see a solid, perhaps even rigid, identity built on her inner solutions to childhood conflict. There are many strengths in Fern's adjustment and much to admire in her. Carrying tremendous professional responsibility and raising two children, she still manages charitable community involvement. Although she is still living with the specter of her father's death, she is much less depressed and desperate than at any other time of her life. She has made a life for herself that realizes her ideals of givingness, and she has become somewhat less dogmatic than she was in college. The growth in Fern has been in small increments. She remains dominated by her moral values and committed to giving to others. She continues to put her own immediate needs, if she is aware of them at all, last. Despite her career and professional involvements, she continues to live a life that is focused on family, on private values, on service.

It seems difficult to make an argument that dire predictions for Fern's life have been borne out. Within the confines of what may be neurotic in her, she has achieved a productive life. She has still not become interested in experimenting with herself or in increasing her experience of life. But, within the boundaries of her sense of duty, she is fulfilled.

Felicia

Felicia in College. Felicia grew up in a suburb of Los Angeles. Her family was well-to-do, her father having graduated from college and become a successful businessman. Her mother had had two years of college and helped her husband part-time after her three children started school. Felicia chose to attend college in New York because that is where her older brother had gone. She was majoring in early childhood education, a field that her parents had chosen for her. She had always loved children, and her parents thought that this field would suit her natural inclinations.

Raised Jewish, Felicia found that religious observance was a way of keeping close to her parents who were so far away. She found herself going to synagogue even more in college than she had at home in order to retain this tie to her family. She reported never having questioned any of her religious beliefs.

Felicia's only political involvements had been to follow her peers' involvements, and these actions were minimal. Her parents were Democrats, but she had little interest in politics.

In regard to sexual standards and values, Felicia said that she was beginning to feel somewhat freer and more relaxed about sex than she had been previously. She said that she would be unable to have premarital intercourse because of her "training" but could now accept it in others. She used to be shocked when friends of hers stayed all night with a guy, and she was unable to talk about sex with anyone. She was proud of being a virgin and answered many of the interviewer's questions in this area by referring to her mother's teachings.

Dominant in Felicia's thoughts when she was interviewed at the end of college were her relationships with others. She said that, in her view, "friends have determined what I am." Preoccupied with how others reacted to her, Felicia was caught up in finding a place with others. In high school, Felicia had felt unable to "connect" with the other girls, who seemed to her to be focused only on themselves and unwilling to open up to others. She saw her peers then as show-offs interested in admiration rather than friendship. Her old friends, the ones from grade school whom she had grown up with, had changed, had gotten involved in drinking and smoking dope, and she refused to go along with them. She had, then, a long period of loneliness in which she became sensitive to being rejected in relationships.

Felicia felt fortunate that she found a roommate in college whom she could look up to as an intelligent and reliable person. From her, she learned something about how to gain acceptance from her peers, and although she felt more popular in college than she had in high school, she continued to worry about how others viewed her.

Although Felicia did not date at all in high school, she found a boyfriend shortly after coming to college. She described him as "a nice guy, sometimes a bit quiet, intelligent." Her mother had counseled her to date others in order to determine whether he was "the one," and Felicia had recently decided that her mother was probably right.

Felicia's family had always been close, and Felicia proudly talked of how she was even closer to her mother now than she had been before she went to college. She described her mother as sensible and practical, trusting of her and eager for her to have the best of everything. Felicia thought her father was finding it hard to let go of her. He treated her more as a child than ever, but Felicia seemed both bemused and happy about this treatment. Her idealization of her family was striking in this interview. She talked of how her parents always treated her and her two brothers absolutely equally. The family was a wonderful, warm, harmonious place. She was unable to criticize anything about her parents, who seemed to her to have been perfect in every way. Felicia had found herself somewhat homesick when she first came to college but felt that it was good for her to learn to cope with new situations that would build her confidence.

One could deduce much about Felicia as she presented herself at the end of college from what she did not say directly. She was clearly a "good" girl, tentatively taking a step away from her parents without really doing it. She was dominated by her need for others' approval, but no one's approval was as important as the esteem of her parents. When she talked about friends or about her boyfriend, they seemed somewhat faceless, as though they were props for her to experience success in relationships, which she could then tell her parents about. She enjoyed calling home and recounting her dates to her mother. At the same time, she had difficulty describing her parents as separate people. She could differentiate them only by describing whom she could take which problems to: problems of relationships to her mother, academic problems to her father. But Felicia was drawing enormous strength from the closeness to her parents. When her friends were doing something she knew her parents would not approve of, her parents were lavish in their praise of her for resisting going along with the crowd. She was consciously struggling with the conflict between her internal standards of behavior and her need for others' approval. She did not want to be rejected by her friends but also could not violate the parentally based inner moral code.

This conflict was evident in a dream Felicia related: "A friend of mine, who is now engaged, snuck out a back door and went out with someone other than her fiance." Felicia interpreted this dream as a punishment for her friend, who rarely let her know where she was going. In this dream are the themes of Felicia's two main personality conflicts: individuation and guilt. We see that consciously Felicia needs to punish the friend for individuating—that is, doing something on her own without telling others. It is also a dream about doing something "bad," something Felicia is unable to do but unconsciously wishes to do.

Felicia was planning to return to Los Angeles when she graduated and to find a teaching job. Her plans for the future were to be teaching and married in five years, to have children and not to be working in ten years.

Throughout this interview, Felicia presented herself as perfect, as a highly confident young woman who knew exactly where she was going and was proud of everything she had ever done. She saw the difficulties she sometimes had as a result of other people's problems and had little insight into herself. At the end of college, Felicia seemed to be a woman who was sure of herself because her parents were sure that she was the person she ought to be. It was clear to the interviewer that not much personal growth had taken place, but Felicia was not looking in this direction.

Felicia at Thirty-Four. Interviewed again twelve years later, Felicia had gone in the occupational direction she had planned. She has taught at the same school for the past eleven years, picking up a master's degree along the way. Teaching has been gratifying for her, and she often imagines that the children she works with are her own. She has remained firm in her religious identity but has had less need for synagogue observance now that she is living close to her family once again.

Until her engagement this past year, the big difficulty in Felicia's life had been finding someone to marry, to complete the other major pole of her life plan. Felicia had been involved in an ambivalent relationship with a man, Len, for six years. He was unable to make a commitment to their relationship, but he provided her some sense of security, and she kept hoping he would finally agree to marry her. "Even when I was dating other people, there was a certain security in knowing that there was someone else in the world who cared about what happened to me." She felt unable to break off this relationship because of the sense that at least some man cared. "When I'm involved in a good, close relationship with someone, I can be a lot more independent because I have that security over there, and I can go off and do other things, and I have someone to tie into. . . . I fear being totally alone. If something happens to me, who is going to be the person that really cares? I used to make Len swear that if there was some sort of national Holocaust, he would come look for me. I had to know that there was one person whose main goal would be to look for me and to take care of me if I were in a time of need."

One insurmountable difficulty in the relationship with Len was severe sexual problems. He was frequently impotent, and she felt unable to cope with it. "I had felt very insecure about my functioning as a woman. I stayed away from sex in most of my relationships." When this problem became intolerable to her, she finally broke off with him.

Shortly afterward, Felicia met Harvey, whom she decided to marry after they dated for three months. She described him as "very compatible" and said that the relationship had brought her comfort and security. "He makes me feel good and wonderful."

The quest for security has emerged as the dominant theme of Felicia's life: how to replace the security she had known in childhood to serve through her adulthood. "I need to know that if I needed another person, there would be a person there for me. I'm a strong person and used to having others depend on me and I need the security of knowing that I too could fall to pieces and have someone there." Felicia became ill several years ago, during a period when Len was away, and her parents canceled their vacation to take care of her. "Thank God I had my parents." She remembered, chillingly, a conversation with her mother that took place during her college years. Her mother had confessed to her that her primary responsibility was her husband and, secondly, her children. "I was absolutely flabbergasted. How could it be that I didn't come first?" The shock of this revelation underlay Felicia's motivation to find someone who would put her first.

At the time of this second interview, Felicia wanted very much to have children (which she did a year later). Felicia said that she always thought she would have to be a wife and mother to feel adult. Throughout her twenties, because she was unmarried and childless, she still felt partly like a young girl. Indeed, Felicia seems to have remained a young girl for quite a long time. When she moved back to California, her intense relationship with her mother continued. Only recently has she begun to question or move away from this near-symbiotic attachment. "I have a regret that I grew up to be such a goody-goody. A lot of my life has been geared to pleasing my mother. And I probably didn't even know that until the past two years. I remember as a child if my mother and I would have a discussion about what I'd wear somewhere, she'd say one thing and I'd say another, and she'd say, 'OK do what you want,' and I would always wear what she said."

Felicia and her mother had major disagreements over Len. Felicia's mother had been full of advice about what she should and should not do. "The few times I stood up to my mother were in regard to this fellow. But I was always afraid of doing something she would not approve of, and what I finally came to realize was that I will always hope to have her support but I will not always have her approval. It was a long time getting to that point. It's only been in the last two years that I've been able to stand up to her." Felicia continues, however, to talk to her mother almost every night and, even when she was engaged to Harvey, listed her mother as the person she felt closest to in the world. Felicia was quick to abandon her career for this new, but long-awaited dream of marriage and family. She feels that a close-knit family gives people direction, as hers did, and that she wants to reexperience that closeness and offer it to her children.

Now that Felicia has found a man to marry, she has begun to be critical of her father. She sees him as having been too passive and not having given her enough verbal or physical affection. With some joy she feels that she has found the man her mother always wanted—a man who would be physically demonstrative and emotionally close to her. Similarly, Felicia talks of the ways she feels she can be a better parent than many of the parents of the children she teaches. Her idealism is renewed and in full force. She wants to be good wife and mother and to never have to be totally alone.

As she reflects on her life history now, Felicia emphasizes once again the struggle to feel accepted and secure. She recalls the sequence of her life as having been a happy time in elementary school, where she had friends and did well, followed by an unhappy time through junior high and high school, where she was too strait-laced and was not accepted by her peers. "I used to go home and cry every night because I was so unhappy."

College was a happy time because she "didn't feel like an oddball." She began opening herself up to others, made friends, began to date. From there, her life was centered around Len and nurturing her students. Only recently has she begun seeing herself as part of the adult world, now that she is on the threshold of marriage.

Felicia has only barely been able to distance and separate herself from an intense symbiotic tie to her mother. She seems to have some conscious awareness of her wish to substitute a husband for her mother, to have a mother who will continue. Although Felicia seems to have made efforts at individuation, in her struggle to buck her mother's disapproval, these efforts have not affected her ongoing fantasy of union with someone. She still has not confronted being alone. Felicia, while externally competent and occupationally successful, internally wants the comfort of mother above all else. She has searched for it everywhere and, at this point in her life, thinks she has found it.

When Felicia talks of the children she hopes to have, she clearly wishes to transfer her symbiosis to the next generation. She imagines that her children will be there to give her affection, to take care of her when she is in need. Once she is a mother, she will have no further need of her work, the main gratification of which seems to have been imagining her importance and centrality to her students. She also will have fulfilled her mother's dream for her: to have everything.

The Foreclosures as a Group

Viewed at the end of college, the Foreclosures' lives were dominated by the effort to feel loved and cared for. Without exception, these women emphasized the closeness of their families and their need for the security they had in them. Their lives after college have been largely an effort to reproduce the warm lovingness they experienced as children.

Of the eight women in this group, all were again classified as Foreclosures twelve years later, indicating relatively little change in identity among the women in this group. The intensive data similarly show little personal growth or inner change. These women appear to live out a dream formed in childhood—a dream that is never questioned, never fundamentally modified.

Of the eight women in this group, all are (or were) in helping or legal professions. The seven who were still working at the time of the interview were in the same occupations they had chosen in college. Their careers have expressed their preoccupation with care of others, but the main focus of their lives has been in their private worlds. Four are married, Felicia is engaged, one is divorced, two are single. All the married Foreclosures have children.

The fate of the Foreclosures in early adulthood seems to rest on their success in finding a mate who fits into their dream of how a family should be. In the structure of their emotional lives, the five married or engaged Foreclosures are very much alike. They all emphasize the centrality of family closeness and harmony, much as they had emphasized these aspects in their families of origin. They are devoted wives and mothers, have few if any conflicts with their husbands, and are centered mainly on their children. One of the never-married women in this group appears to be a shy, limited, Fundamentalist Christian whose life is organized around Bible study and friends of similar orientation. At age thirty-four, she remains a virgin but is still hoping to find a man to marry. The other unmarried woman has a history almost exactly like Felicia's. Despite being a highly successful lawyer, she is growing increasingly despondent about her failure to find a suitable mate.

Ironically, perhaps, the greatest personal growth among the Foreclosure group was found in the divorced woman. The failure of her dream, precipitated largely by her husband's decision to end the marriage, caused her to develop internally. But even this failure did not force revision of her fundamental orientation. She is unable to see how she may have contributed to the difficulties in the relationship, and although she did come to terms with being on her own, she is still looking for a man. "I would not like to think of myself as the type of woman who needs a man, however unappealing he may be, rather than be by myself. But I don't want to give up my hopes for a family." Although this woman has one of the most distinguished careers in the entire sample, she is unable to envision a life different from the one she had as a child.

Foreclosure women are hardworking, responsible, and capable, and for these reasons have been highly successful in their careers. Nevertheless, career success is never as satisfying to them as being loved. These women will give up prestigious, gratifying jobs without a second thought to follow husbands and fiances to other states. Security, the main quest of the Foreclosures, is found in relationships not in work.

Foreclosures are not insightful women, nor do they enjoy emotional upheaval. They approach all aspects of their lives with a startling lack of ambivalence: Things are all good or all bad. As one Foreclosure woman, from a rural background, put it, "I enjoy a quiet life like my family. I was pretty unworldly with my upbringing, which I think is good. I'm conservative and helpful, which are qualities my parents developed in me. I'm different [from my parents] because I'm more open-minded and less critical of others."

The lives of these Foreclosure women offer some counsel to the debate that has been waged in the psychological literature concerning the adaptiveness of the Foreclosure status for women. Puzzled by the consistent differences between male and female Foreclosures, some investigators have suggested that the difference is only superficial. Perhaps Foreclosure women, despite their apparent strength and solidity of character structure, are building an identity on a fairly infantile ego organization and show few deep signs of psychological health (Ginsburg and Orlofsy, 1981; Josselson, 1982).

Research efforts along these lines have been fruitful in showing that the Foreclosure emphasis on security and safety reflects some fixation at an early stage of psychological development. As a result, these women bypass the adolescent task of individuation. Our root assumption in developmental psychology is that circumventing this important stage will cause such women to be less successful than Achievements or Moratoriums in negotiating the developmental tasks of adulthood. They would likely be less flexible and resilient and less able to cope with adult demands.

The Foreclosure women in this study, viewed twelve years after college, show a unique pattern of personality development, but they are not less adjusted than the others and they do not have more symptoms or evidence of psychological disturbance. They are somewhat more likely than the other groups to have had short-term psychotherapy, generally related to problems in relationships. They are also more likely than any of the other groups to have advanced (post-bachelor's) degrees. The data from this study are consistent with those of Mallory (1983), who, in a long-term psychometric study, found no evidence that Foreclosure women were more maladjusted or less mature than others.

Foreclosure women, then, cannot be simplistically characterized. They cling to others, but they are strivers. Their universe is somewhat narrow, yet they contribute to society. Their lives are shaped by a strong sense of duty. They do what they have learned is right to do and repress or disavow their own impulses. Their lives are dominated by a strong sense of family, tradition, and moral values.

In their ripening adulthood, they have become much like their families of origin even though social-class circumstances may have changed a bit through upward mobility. They have so strongly internalized their parents' values and patterns that they are indistinguishable from them. The Foreclosures represent a form of growth through identification rather than individuation. That is, they grow by taking in, ever more completely, aspects of their adored parents rather than through self-discovery and increasing differentiation.

What early factors may presage such a developmental pattern? Looking now at retrospective and clinical data collected while these women were in college, one finds that without exception Foreclosure women were focused on the closeness of their families and the security they had in them. Their developmental concerns seemed to center on allying themselves with someone who could do everything and protect them from everything—a person much like one or both of their parents. To them life was a process of pleasing some powerful other in order to maintain the emotional supplies they needed for living. From the earliest time, being a very good girl for very good parents was a source of self-esteem. In time, this representation of the very good parents became internalized, and these women had only to continue to please this inner ideal to feel safe, loved, and secure.

Such a sequence is understood to be the universal pattern of development. It is a way of describing the internalization of the superego, a process that all normally developing children undergo. Among Foreclosures, however, this constellation of personality organization never gets reworked. Whereas at adolescence most people redo the ego/superego balance and, in so doing, internalize other ideals, throw off some childhood prohibitions, and become more ego directed rather than superego dominated, the Foreclosures do not. In a sense, they avoid adolescence and carry forward into adulthood the same selves they were as children.

Throughout childhood, these selves—these identities—are ascribed. One is assigned a family, a school, a set of expectations from parents and teachers. One may comply or rebel, but one can rarely change the ascription. Nor can the child imagine changing these givens, trusting as children are wont to do that the world is as it should be. Only in adolescence, with increased cognitive and emotional resources, do separation and individuation from parents make possible the serious question of how to invest aspects of one's identity that have been liberated from prior, childhood-determined ways of being.

Whereas children gain self-esteem through pleasing parents and internalized parents ("being good"), adolescents can increasingly set and attempt to meet their own standards, independently of the responses of the social world. As the rigid, moralistic superego of childhood gives way to the more flexible, reality-oriented ego control of late adolescence and adulthood, the person becomes increasingly able to internally regulate self-esteem.

Traditional psychoanalytic theory has emphasized the achievement of autonomy, of emancipation from parents, as the central developmental task of adolescence. Blos (1962) characterized adolescence as a phase in which aspects of self still enmeshed in the parents are differentiated and made autonomous. Other theorists stress disengagement from infantile object ties (Josselyn, 1952; Freud, 1958; Spiegel, 1958), repudiation of parental ego support (Balser, 1957; Blos, 1967), and discarding of identification with parents (Josselyn, 1954). In short, classical theory has stressed the separation and individuation that occur in adolescence, the growth away from childhood ties that frees the young person to make new investments, find new objects, develop new identifications. The ensuing portrait is reminiscent of the American heroic ideal, the lone frontiersman, without ties, seeking to build a new life and a better world.

Studies of normal adolescents, however, provide a quite different portrait (Douvan and Adelson, 1966; Offer, 1969;

Offer, Ostrov, and Howard, 1981). Most adolescents, male and female, maintain quite harmonious and warm relationships with parents throughout their adolescence. To be sure, there are tiffs about rules, dress, and music playing. Individuation proceeds through irritating the parents to delineate oneself from them, but the battles tend not to be major ones. Nor is there any evidence, among normal adolescents, of abrogation of the parents or denial of them. The healthiest adolescents wish to maintain a loving connection to their parents, may call home frequently even while away at college, and continue to show concern about not damaging their relationships with their parents. In an effort to understand the theoretically necessary separation-individuation that takes place during adolescence, our theory has failed to conceptualize the continuing connection and relatedness that also occur. The adolescent is not a lone frontiersman. Rather, he or she is an adventurer with an accompanying cortege, internally and externally. And this cortege can have more or less influence in shaping the young person's identity.

In Erikson's original conceptualization, the Foreclosed position is one from which all adolescents begin the quest for identity. Research has, indeed, shown a general decrease in the incidence of Foreclosure identities through the college years (Waterman, 1982). One has the sense, in interviewing a college-age Foreclosure, that this developmental position is poised for change, like a bud awaiting suitable sunlight to open. When I interviewed these women as seniors in college, my clinical/developmental mind wondered what would shake them into a new path and when, what would throw cogs into their certain wheels, would force them to look at themselves and see that they have choices. The follow-up data, however, suggest that college may be the critical period for identity formulation to begin. Those whose investment in bypassing the developmental task of adolescence is so strong as to resist the heterogeneous influences of the college environment, whose determination to avoid exploration is so stubborn as to survive college with blinders on, are unlikely to encounter growth-promoting forces of equal magnitude later on.

Approaching midlife, these women do not foresee fundamental alterations. In fact, the only changes they can imagine are dire ones: deaths of loved ones, illnesses. They do not speak of unrealized aspects of themselves. Nor would adventure be any more welcome to them than it has ever been. Their ironclad identities, hardened by the end of college, become only more solidified through early adulthood. There is no internal push for change. It is difficult to imagine the external circumstances that could lead them to rework or rethink, especially when they manage to have their lives work so well. As a result, it appears that although, for some, Identity Foreclosure is a developmental beginning, for others, those who remain Foreclosures at the end of college, it becomes a way of life.

What, then, might explain the reluctance to explore with the self that presages Identity Foreclosure? One important aspect of adolescent development is that of peer support. The need for ego support from peers derives from the loosening of ego ties to the parents. Peer support provides the bulwark from which to rework the superego, to form new identifications, and to shake loose from dependence on the parents. Among the Foreclosures, however, attempts at meaningful relationships with peers continually fail. The Foreclosures are unable to establish enough trust outside the family for friendships to form.

Like Fern and Felicia, all the Foreclosure women show some history of difficulties in peer relationships. They felt different, rejected, or isolated as children or as early adolescents and were thrown on their families. Many of them had parents who were mistrustful of the outside world, who taught them, in effect, never to trust strangers, that only the family could be counted on. Fern's mother, for example, allowed her daughter to retreat after her first encounter with hostility in the outside world. Felicia's mother, afraid that her daughter would be corrupted by schoolmates, provided her daughter with massive support to resist whatever the high school crowd did.

Foreclosure women, then, appear to have had mothers who were both possessive and themselves fearful and isolated. They may have passed on to their daughters their own fears of rejection and mistrust of others. The ensuing pact, "I love you and you love me and the rest of the world be damned," provides a highly gratifying source of narcissistic supplies for the developing girl and obviates the need to seek other relationships. Several Foreclosure women were the "good" child in a family with an identifiable "bad" child. They saw themselves, then, as doubly having to be "good," to make up for the badness of the other child, to be a comfort to the parents.

Most of these women also report having had intensely affectionate relationships with fathers during childhood. As college women, Foreclosures appear to have the sense of being loved by the perfect man, whom they could not imagine displeasing.

The upsurge of sexual interest that often forms a rift in the harmonious family relations of late childhood does not occur in the adolescence of these women. They deal with sexual impulses largely through guilt and repression. Pleasure results from being good, not from sexual gratification. Sexuality, then, at adolescence, is seen as being a part of the re-creation of a secure, protecting environment. Foreclosures do not experiment sexually. Rather, they choose a heterosexual partner who is a simple substitute for one or the other parent, and they choose him because he offers security or protection. As one woman, during college, described her boyfriend of three years, "He's just something to cling to." Another woman, at age thirty-four, describing her decision to marry her boyfriend of eight years, said, "We were like a couple of old shoes."

Foreclosure women have difficulty forming relationships with peers of both genders because their moral standards are so demanding, their expectations so exacting. In a sense, they do to others what they experienced their parents as doing to them: setting high and rigid standards, insisting on prescribed behavior. Having not differentiated themselves or achieved awareness of their own internal contradictions, they relate to others, especially to their men, by trying to make them fit their preconceived ideas. They are judgmental rather than empathic. One Foreclosure woman had a major crisis in her life when she discovered her husband having an affair, an affair that he sheepishly and apologetically relinquished. With the help of their priest, he was brought back into line. Seven years later, however, this woman continues to be unable to understand his motivations, nor does she care to. He did something bad; she has tried to forget it and to forgive him. But he robbed her, forever, of her sense of the perfection of their marriage. Foreclosure women have clear and uncompromising specifications for a potential husband and, once married, ongoing prescriptions for required behavior. Because they cannot understand their own irrational selves, because they cannot experience wishes or ambivalence or inner conflict, they have a hard time appreciating the complexity of another. They can demand and they can love and support, but they cannot understand. It appears that Foreclosures are likely to marry somewhat passive men who share their commitment to required behavior. Or else they find men so uncertain about their own identities that they relish having a woman tell them how to live their lives.

At the end of college, Foreclosures typically were not able to describe their parents as separate or differentiated human beings. They tended to describe them in idealized, somewhat empty terms. A fairly typical college-age Foreclosure description of family of origin is the following: "My family was always very close and family oriented. They never pressured us or pounced on us or told us what to do. They were always fair and reasonable." Foreclosures are frightened more than anything of expressing anger or dissatisfaction with their parents, as though doing so would destroy the ideal protector they so desperately need. To admit that parents are flawed, that they have limitations, is to risk being alone in a hostile world without the omnipotent other to keep one safe.

Foreclosures also seem to have a deeply held idea that other people make you what you are. With this inner psychological template they construe human personality. They have little sense of a self creating itself. So it feels right and sensible that they are a creation and clone of their parents. Isn't everyone? The childhood assumption that they would some day take their parent's place seems to be held as a matter of loyalty. When they see alternatives that appeal to them, they feel as though they are betraying or going against their parents. Asked to tell a Thematic Apperception Test story about a picture of a

girl standing with books in the foreground while older adults do
farm work in the background behind her, one woman produced
the following description: "Perhaps she thinks it's a lot of hard
work, I'm not sure she's despondent or thinks it's too much
work. She's not rejecting the life of her parents. She's dressed
well enough, she would like to better herself, but she's not looking down on that type of life." Notice that most of the words in
this story are used to deny feelings, to ward off the unacceptable thoughts that nevertheless immediately come to mind. The
underlying anxiety in this story, which appears in one way or
another in all the Foreclosures, is that to be different is to criticize.

As adults in their early thirties, these women continue to
describe their families of origin in glowing terms, perhaps even
more so than they did while they were in college. Whatever bits
of adolescent discord might have existed have been forgotten
by this time, and Foreclosure women experience their gratitude
and indebtedness to their families for their solid foundation.

Not surprisingly, adult Foreclosures describe their husbands in much the same way. "I knew him for as long as I can
remember. He had a good sense of humor, we had many common friends, the same religious background, he had a nice family, and he made me feel emotionally like a big deal." Asked in
what ways she and her husband complement each other, another Foreclosure woman said, "We work well together in the
kitchen. We both like to cook, and he helps around the house.
He satisfies my romantic and sentimental needs. We respect
each other—anticipate each other's needs and are always there
for each other."

As adults, Foreclosures remain close to their families of
origin, especially to their mothers. Asked to list the people they
feel closest to, in order, Foreclosures are most likely to list husband, then children, then mother. Few of them have had or
maintain close friendships outside their families. Those who
have had friends are disappointed by the transiency of friendship, feel hurt or rejected when friends drift away, and retreat
again to the predictability and certainty of family closeness.
Throughout their lives, Foreclosures maintain their sensitivity

to rejection, and such sensitivity becomes a central organizing theme of their lives. They treasure the safe and predictable because they guard a long memory of what it feels like to be wounded.

Foreclosures are not emotionally complex women, and perhaps for this reason psychologists who have written about them tend to be deprecating. They experience little inner conflict or ambivalence. They tend to speak in idealized tones, emphasizing the rightness of everything. They have a goal or goals and are marching down their chosen roads without looking around or considering other possibilities. Their certitude and self-assurance are enviable.

The fact that they have careers and are so successful is perhaps surprising unless one remembers their orientation to being good. They seek success and will bring to striving all their considerable resources. Stoicism, single-mindedness, and self-assurance keep them focused on their goals. That they are working and mothering at the same time—different from their mothers' experience—seems to cause them little difficulty. Many emphasize that their mothers are proud of them, thus reassuring themselves that their working is all right. For several, financial necessity is a strong incentive to continue working, but they do not bemoan this necessity too much. They do not experience career/family conflict because they always put the family first.

The Foreclosure pattern of development seems to describe the popular though now out-of-favor notion of women as culture bearers. Having deeply internalized the values of their parents, remaining attached to the religion they were raised in, finding men who will carry on their traditions, these women carry forward into their adult lives the emotional warmth and security of their childhoods. Many of them list as one of the accomplishments of which they are thus far most proud owning their own house. Indeed, they are building nests at this point in their lives. And their sense of themselves, their identities, and their self-esteem derive from the success of their nest building.

Chapter 5

  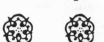

Pavers of
the Way:
The Identity Achievements

Two roads diverged in a wood, and I—
I took the one less traveled by
And that has made all the difference.
—*Robert Frost,* "The Road Not Taken"

The Identity Achievements are a far more diverse group than the Foreclosures and share less psychological commonality. A redundant pattern leads to Identity Foreclosure, but many factors and circumstances result in the formulation of a self-made identity. When we meet Alice, Andrea, and Amanda, they may not seem on the surface to be different from the Foreclosures, but they have forged their identities in quite a different way. These women have separated themselves from their childhood ties and formed individuated, distinct identities.

Psychological growth at adolescence involves not only increasing autonomy from the parents but also increased individuation from the aspects of the parents that have become part of the preadolescent self. The newly adolescent girl does not just obey her parents. In an important sense, she is her parents. She has internalized their values, their prohibitions, their priorities, and their ways of being in the world. Further growth, then, implies not just doing things away from their supervision but re-working her internal self. This is the process of individuation. Physical and emotional separation from parents does not neces-sarily imply that individuation has occurred. Younger college students, for example, living away from home, often make choices, quite consciously, based on their perception of their parents' choices. Their feeling, or wish perhaps, is that parents do know best. This is the process we witnessed in the Fore-closures.

Separation is painful because it involves giving up known comforts for uncertain and unpredictable new ones. It means loss of the loved and familiar and entails a certain amount of mourning. Although the adolescent gains in autonomy and free-dom, she pays for it by relinquishing the security and protec-tion she had as a child in the sheltering arms of her family.

Individuation is painful in another way, a perhaps more intense and difficult way. Because individuation involves giving up trusted aspects that feel like the self, the adolescent is sub-ject to the anxiety of uncertainty, a sense of rootlessness. In return the adolescent gains possibility. But freedom can be ter-rifying. Many late adolescents who have successfully individ-uated look back somewhat wistfully at the assurance they felt when younger. Then, they say, they were sure what to believe, they knew what was right and what wrong, they would simply follow the orbit of life their parents had created for themselves, and everything would somehow turn out all right. Now, by con-trast, they feel the relativity and risk inherent in life's decisions. They are free but vulnerable.

In the process of development, it is at this point that identity formation makes its most apparent and dramatic en-trance. When aspects of the self are freed from their connection to parental identifications, they become available to fundamen-tally change and reorganize the sense of identity. If we are look-ing at how the young adult hatches out of the child, we are con-cerned with understanding the separation-individuation process. But if we are interested in what the new adult does with aspects liberated in the personality, we are in the realm of identity for-mation. However, the two processes are intricately intertwined.

Those aspects of the self that are wrested free are reshaped and modified, new elements are added and mixed together with older, unindividuated aspects of self, resulting in the integration of a new identity.

Identity Achievement women have gone through this process during adolescence. They have forged identities on their own terms, having examined and reworked the identities assigned to them as children. They are not necessarily achievers in the work world, a fact that often confuses people who may think that to have achieved an identity a woman must also achieve in a career. Rather, they are women who choose lives after sifting through options, amalgamating aspects of who they were with whom they choose to become, and, in so doing, have a sense of following a life plan they can claim as their own.

The eight women in this group do not differ dramatically from the Foreclosures in the dailiness of their lives. Six of them are married; four have children. All of them are working in some employment outside the home. It is in their psychological structures not in the contents of their lives that they differ from the Foreclosures. Seven of the eight have remained Identity Achievements from college age into early adulthood, although all have made further changes in their lives. One woman, rated as Identity Achievement in college, has returned to a Moratorium state, questioning her choices and trying to make new ones.

There are subtle, yet important, differences between the Identity Achievements and the Foreclosures despite their surface similarity. The Identity Achievements are, in general, more flexible, more open to experience, more firmly rooted in an internal sense of self, and, hence, more independent of external sources of self-esteem. These differences, largely differences of degree, nevertheless rest on different patterns of inner psychological functioning.

Alice

Alice in College. Alice was an attractive woman from a small town in Pennsylvania. With the intention of becoming a physical therapist, she chose a large private university with a program that met her interests. She wanted the chance to live in Philadelphia, to "see what it was like," wishing to taste experience outside the confines of the small town she had seldom been away from. Her parents had had no specific plans for her, but, since childhood, she had given a great deal of thought to what she might become. Once, she thought she might like to be a veterinarian, then later felt attracted by the idea of being a teacher. Her high school guidance counselor told her about the field of physical therapy and took her to a rehabilitation hospital so that she could witness for herself the kind of work that could be done. Alice felt an immediate calling. Most of her high school classmates were headed for the local community college, and Alice, who was engaged to be married as a senior in high school, assumed that she would do likewise and become a physical therapy assistant. But something seemed unfair about this plan. She had done so well in school that she felt that she would be cheating herself. So she decided to break the mold and apply to a four-year college.

In her religious life, Alice's primary struggle was with her belief in God. She remained uncertain that the God of her childhood was a reality but continued to wish that there were "someone to go to for help." She felt unable to know what to believe and considered herself, therefore, an agnostic. She continued, however, to study many religions in order to "see if I can put together things I can accept." Although she had strong political opinions, schoolwork kept her too busy in college to be able to participate in political action.

In regard to sex, Alice went through a number of distinct phases of change. At the end of high school, she had a strict set of standards in regard to virginity that, during the summer following her first year of college, she totally abandoned. For a time after breaking up with her high school boyfriend, she indulged in indiscriminate sexuality. Although she rationalized her behavior to herself at the time, she later found this sexual freedom to be incompatible with her standards for self-respect. This realization led to her belief, at the time of the interview, that for her, sex was permissible only in the context of a loving relationship.

In Alice, one sees the typical Identity Achievement pattern of identity commitments following periods of crisis or re-thinking. She did not make her decisions automatically, based on childhood conviction, but rather left possibilities open, changed her mind, experimented a bit before deciding. At the same time, Alice appeared, at the end of college, to be committed to the decisions she had made. She was clear on an occupational path, was still struggling with religious belief, was thinking hard about political issues, and had chosen a set of sexual values.

A reflective woman who seemed remarkably mature and self-possessed, Alice had relished her college experience for the lessons in living she had derived from it. She described herself as always having been more of a leader than a follower. She always had high standards for herself, and, as a child, she thought it particularly important to get high grades, to be in plays, and to play baseball well. Her sole sibling, an older brother, was also successful, and Alice always felt it crucial to do at least as well as he. The satisfaction she got from achievements seemed to her, as she looked back on her growing up years, to have been paramount in her life from the time she started school. "When I was in high school, I was the honor-society, cheerleader, student-council type. When I came to college, I went overboard, to the other extreme, but I learned from it."

In the town where she grew up, few girls went to college. Like many of her classmates, she was engaged during her senior year of high school. However, the importance of academic achievement in her life caused her to have serious misgivings about immediate marriage, and she decided to postpone it and apply to college. Her fiance, who had been her steady boyfriend for six years, remained in the town and took a job, waiting for her. Within a year, Alice felt that she had changed so much that they had little basis for continuing their relationship. The trauma caused by giving up a person who had been so important to her for so long led Alice to "go wild" and throw off, experimentally, all the vestiges of the person she had been. This experiment led her into drugs as well as promiscuity until she discovered the core of those things that mattered to her. At the time of the college interview, she was deeply involved in her career goals and in a relationship with a man whom she thought she might marry at some point, although marriage was a frightening idea at that time.

While in college, Alice had been doing volunteer work in a rehabilitation hospital and found this work extremely gratifying. "There's nothing like it," she said emphatically, "getting someone up on their feet for the first time after a ruinous accident. It's really a very selfish occupation, but I couldn't have chosen a more satisfying one." Alice was looking forward to having a real job in the field and, with something of a shudder of fear, spoke of the bad decision not going to college would have been; she would have condemned herself to being an assistant and missed out on the joys of being truly helpful to others.

As she saw her life at the end of college, she was eager to work in her field: "to be on my own for awhile, to do things and see things before I settle down." Her work was of primary importance to her. She seemed also to have already thought through her plans for a family. She disapproved of some women in her class who had children and left them all day with their mothers. When she had children, although that was many years off, Alice felt strongly that she would want to give them the mother's attention that they need. She would not work when they were small but would later resume part-time work during the hours they were in school.

Alice described her parents as having been loving but distant. From her description, they seem to have been rather American Gothic in flavor—hard-working people who were proud of her accomplishments but never got overinvolved or interfered with her life. Her mother she saw as passive and withdrawn, and Alice wished for greater closeness to her. Her father was the disciplinarian in the family; Alice felt that he was always reasonable but set definite limits. Although she never felt particularly close to him either, she did feel that he was the parent from whom she had to win her independence. The battle was fought the summer of her junior year of college when she planned to go to Europe but had to go over her father's protests.

As she thought about her parents, Alice became somewhat saddened by her distance from them. "I never really knew my parents. My father always came home from work, ate supper, read the paper, watched TV. My mother is very hesitant about meeting people and doing things. It's not that there wasn't love there, but we never did much as a family. One day in my sophomore year of college, I went home and said to them, 'Do you realize I really don't know much about you— your values, your ideas. what you think.' And the reaction I got, especially from my mother, was 'OK, what do you want to know?' And I asked some questions, and she'd give me a five-word answer. Coming to school and hearing the other girls who discuss everything with their mother, I realized there was something lacking. I just couldn't." Alice was aware, however, of an intense wish for them to be proud of her.

Because Alice's parents seemed to have expected her to be independent from a relatively early age, Alice always hungered for nurturance. Her intense needs "to be perfect" and to be accomplished were partly in the service of her attempt to win interest and love from them. Failing to do so, she transformed her successes into gratifications in their own right. Alice was thus able to defend herself against her dependent longings by becoming a leader and being a success. She was also able to salve the feelings of deprivation by making friends. With little activity at home, Alice turned to her peers for closeness and interest. The one dream that she reported echoed the theme that people can make up for disappointments: "It was my girlfriend's birthday party and somehow her cake got smashed. Then her boyfriend came and she was happy again."

Alice's pattern was to make up for her feelings of disappointment by immersing herself in a relationship with a man. At the age of twelve, she began the relationship with the boy to whom she was later engaged, a relationship that lasted nearly seven years. He promised to fulfill her needs for parenting in that he "made a groove for me to fit into" and was demanding of her. Although she had other friends during this period, her boyfriend was paramount in her life, and he set definite standards against which she could continually test herself. Her breaking away from him after her first year of college was a symbolic break with the self she had been for him and an abandonment of the need for the neat, ordered, and intense authority to which she had become accustomed.

At the end of this period of her life, Alice turned to her own abilities and to other friends for self-esteem. This time, however, she tried to be more realistic in both areas. In her work, she struggled with tempering her ideals. Once she had wished she could "help everyone for free," but she had experiences that forced her to admit to herself that she had a streak of selfishness. Here, she was wrestling with giving up the ideal of perfection as total self-sacrifice and to acknowledge and integrate some of her own needs. She also became less idealistic in regard to relationships and realized how demanding she had been of her boyfriends in wanting them to be "perfect" men. In the serious relationship she was then involved in, there was more space for both of them than she had ever experienced before. Both were tolerant of the other's wishes, interests, and needs.

Although Alice was becoming more realistic in regard to her parents by the end of college, she was still experiencing the old wishes for closeness, this time in the form of hoping to take good care of them in their old age. In many ways, Alice appeared to be attempting to mourn the ultimate loss of what she never had—closeness to her parents—and the resultant depression was not far below the surface. She felt keenly aware of the fact that her parents' image of her did not match what she was, and while she longed to tell them about some of her less conventional experiences, she felt that they could not understand. Although she said that they never had definite expectations for her, she seemed to have identified with them just enough so that being so different from them was, at least unconsciously, a betrayal of them. She saw her parents as quiet people who, while not outstanding, at least did no wrong, and it had been a joy of her childhood to feel their pride in her, to hear them boast about her to others.

As a result, Alice, at the end of college, was bearing a strong sense of guilt. Her nagging sense of having somehow betrayed her parents lent an edge of pain to her otherwise careful and optimistic exterior. Clearly she had won her independence by denying, rather than integrating, her needs to be dependent. Although she had changed too much to continue to love her high school boyfriend, underneath she still missed him. Alice's maturation resided in growing forward nonetheless, giving up aspects that were gratifying but not growth promoting, even if doing so involved suffering. Relinquishing these old forms of self-esteem meant a continuing need to reassure herself of her independence, of her competence, and she seemed on the trail of a new form of personality organization.

Most striking about Alice was the effectiveness of her defenses and coping mechanisms. At times, she appeared quite anxious and rather depressed, but she seemed to have been able to utilize her capacities and her relationships to guard against these negative feelings. She also felt a great deal of control over her own life and responsibility for the decisions she was making.

Alice at Thirty-Two. At age thirty-two, Alice remained vivacious and attractive. As she had planned, she became a physical therapist and feels she has been a good one. Alice's work has been rewarding in the challenges and satisfactions it involves. Her present job is frustrating, however, because of the administrative responsibilities she has assumed within the agency. Recently, she has begun feeling bored with her job; she often sees it as no more to her than a paycheck. For five years she made efforts to improve the situation at work but finally gave up because no one else seemed to care. This situation is demoralizing enough that she has begun taking courses in speech therapy, preparing for a career change. At present, she is job sharing, working three days per week because of her family, which is her first priority. She and her husband are also thinking about starting a small business together. "It would be nice to be self-sufficient and not have to work for anyone else."

Alice is not religious. She attends church for social reasons, largely because her husband wishes her to. She plans to raise their children in his Catholic religion but intends to let them know that her beliefs are different and to expose them to a variety of religions.

Alice continues to be interested in politics and now has

time to devote herself to causes that are important to her. She has worked actively on local environmental issues. She considers herself to be more of a feminist now than ten years ago, more of an isolationist (both in attitude toward national policy and in her personal life-style), and more fiscally conservative now that she's a taxpayer.

She continues to hold liberal, thoughtful views about sex. She is open to possibilities. Although she and her husband have an exclusive, monogamous relationship, she considers it imaginable that in the distant future they might agree to experiment with relationships outside their marriage.

Twelve years after college, then, Alice, in her identity formation, remains committed and clear on her choices but not blinded to other alternatives. She retains the quality of committing herself to something "for the foreseeable future," aware that she or circumstances may change. Full of vitality and reflectiveness, Alice continues to pay attention to her sense of growing.

Just after graduation from college, Alice met Richard, whom she married two months later. With the relative structure of college life over, Alice, more frightened of her freedom than she had expected to be, promptly fell in love. She describes Richard now as having been a nice guy but basically a loser. He was semialcoholic and frequently unemployed, and when he began to grow violent, Alice walked out. The years of this marriage she now views as one of the most stressful times of her life. Shortly after the wedding, she began to see aspects of Richard she had blinded herself to previously, but she hoped that by taking care of him, she could win love and stability. Needing to hide her unhappiness from her friends and family, she withdrew from them and escaped into her work. Unwilling to give up on the marriage and admit she made a mistake, Alice tried for three years to make it work. She thinks now that she stayed much longer than she need have. Throughout this chaotic marriage, her work had a stabilizing effect on her. As she had at other times in her life, Alice turned to her own competence for self-esteem. But once again, after their divorce, she found herself alone and frightened.

When she met Adam, just a few months after her divorce, she approached him with great caution. She saw him as a companion with whom to share good times, but she was reluctant to get involved. She discovered in him, however, "the most compatible man I have ever known," and they married three years later in a private ceremony they wrote themselves. They moved then to a small town in West Virginia, where they could work with the poor and enjoy the pleasures of living in the country. Of her five-year marriage, she says, "We can effectively combine our energies toward common goals. We work jointly in childcare, household management, earning income, rebuilding the house, growing our own food. We also play together well. Any clashes we have are minor and temporary. I'm at peace. I have a wonderful family and my own house, which were major goals in my life. I have a life partner with whom I hope to grow old."

Alice's current life is bounded by the demands of two children under the age of two. Age thirty had been a now-or-never crisis for her. Although for most of her twenties Alice had not wanted to have children, she now looks on motherhood as "a precious addition to my life, and I would have been foolish not to experience it." Her children have added immense joy and love to her life, but she feels that her personal endeavors have had to take a back seat for awhile. She is aware of the costs of motherhood but does not regret her choice: "The most difficult [part] has been the lack of time—to be with friends, to read, to write a letter, to go to the bathroom, etc. I especially miss having time alone with Adam. I wish I had as much time and energy to devote to being a wife as I have to being a mother. And the same amount again to devote to just being a woman. Oh, well. I know this is a temporary situation, so I can deal with it."

Economically, Alice and her family are living somewhat sparsely, but she does not feel in need of anything. She has been healthy, does not smoke or drink, but smokes marijuana socially on occasion.

Alice's main investment is in realizing the bucolic dream that she and Adam share. She wants them to spend more time with their son and daughter than her parents did with her. She would also like her children to be feminists, meaning that they recognize that women are the equals of men. Despite the pressures and strains of her life, Alice appears to be, in a deep way, content. Of her hopes for the future, she says, "I hope Adam and I can grow old and comfortable in our own home and become as self-sufficient as possible. I hope we see our children prosper and grow into happy, contented adults. I hope to have the opportunity to seek various personal endeavors, continuing my education, getting into some type of craft seriously, to continue skiing and hiking as long as possible. I'm happy with myself as I am now (except for a few rough edges). I don't want to be a significantly different person. I like me as I am now. I suppose it would be nice to be wiser, more patient, and have more serenity in my life—and I expect those will come with time."

Summarizing her life, Alice says, "My most important accomplishment has been being a 'good' wife and mother. Leaving behind two happy, healthy, intelligent people to the world would be a significant contribution. I also feel positive about the people I've helped in my work and hope to do more. I don't expect to make the history book's pages, nor do I care to. I wish to be contented. I am now and expect to be when I'm eighty. That's all that really matters, isn't it?"

Looking back on the chapters of her life, Alice demarcates the eras by the men she had relationships with. Although the theme of her academic and work successes remains strong, Alice nevertheless has felt most anchored and defined by the significant man in her life.

Alice has, therefore, continued the pattern evident in her college interview. Her ambition remains counterpoised against her need for relationship. Although her relationships have progressively become less dependent, more tailored to meeting her unique needs, she nevertheless defines contentment in terms of mutuality and love. She seems able to take joy in her obvious talents only when she expresses them in the context of such a relationship.

As an adult, Alice continues to have a distant, affectionate relationship with her parents. Her conflicts about independence from them seem to have been resolved long ago. She feels that from her father she got her brains and her tendency to hide within herself during emotional times. From her mother she got her domestic skills and her temper. She feels that she is more extroverted and assertive than either parent. Alice keenly feels the advantage over them that her college education gave her but uses this advantage to understand them rather than to judge them. "I never got close to my parents. It's not that there wasn't love there. I just never knew anything about their lives, their values, and opinions." Although these were much the same words that Alice had used in college, they were now uttered in a matter-of-fact tone, without the old note of longing. Clearly, Alice has accepted her differences from them and is eager to redefine life in her own terms, without a need to see herself as carrying on the family tradition. Because she was not close to her parents, however, the first order of business in Alice's life has continually been that of finding someone to be close to. Men have served her in this way, from her high school boyfriend, who "made a groove for me to fit into," to Adam, who shares and supports her bucolic dream. In short, one can say that Alice has clearly individuated from her family, even though her identity formation is marked by the need to counterpoise her identity elements against those of a man.

Alice never did realize the goal she stated in college of doing things and seeing things and being on her own before she settled down. Fear got the best of her after she left college. When she met Richard, she fell intensely in love with him, overlooking his problematic, trouble-ridden side, and hung on to him for some structure in her life. In Adam, she found a man who would accept and nurture her individuality. By her early adulthood, Alice's dreams of independent adventure have been forgotten, having been compromised, at last, with her needs for a secure relationship.

Among the Identity Achievements, Alice presents the most clearly defined picture of identity testing, exploration, false starts, and new routes chosen. For the others, the development in identity and individuality is less visible, less identifiable. It is harder to say, "Here is an identity-exploring moment." Growth and development among these other women take place, as it were, inside, under the skin. One day, as they look back, they can see that they have traveled in significant ways far from home, or far from the selves they were, but they had little awareness of the voyage. For these women, the import of identity-modifying experiences tends to be muted or not perceived while they are occurring. It is as if the woman says to herself, "Well, I'm doing something different, but it doesn't change me. I'm still the same person." With an accumulation of these something differents comes less need to retreat to a familiar shore. The differences become reliable and come to feel like a part of the self. The sensation of change, then, occurs after it has already happened, after it is too late to change back.

Andrea

Andrea in College. When interviewed in college, Andrea was a tense and intense woman who was uncomfortable talking about herself. This discomfort seemed to be less a product of reticence than of a habit of mind not to look deeply in the mirror often.

Andrea planned to go to medical school. Her father had encouraged her interest in science, a field she particularly enjoyed because it was "hard and a challenge." She maintained some contact with the Catholicism of her childhood but allied herself with a newer, less conventional practice of the faith. Politically, she was involved in local campaigns, had strong political opinions. She felt sex to be permissible in the context of a strong commitment to a person, and although she knew her parents would vociferously disagree, she felt that "that's the way they are and I'm different." On the criteria of crisis and commitment in the categories of occupation, religion, politics, and sexual standards, Andrea was clearly an Identity Achievement.

A goal-oriented woman, Andrea decided on her course in life through a fairly gradual process of consolidating independence. She portrayed her family as having been close and overprotective but important to her because of the many experiences they shared together. Her father was the source of her intellectual interests, and she fondly remembered the hours they spent discussing what she was learning in school. She struggled more with her mother, primarily over hours and friends and other issues of freedom.

Until she went to college, Andrea felt she was a lot like her parents; she had their morality and their religion and their values of hard work and success. She had few friends during her school years because her peers considered her to be "the studious one." Attending Catholic schools, she grew up without serious challenge to her parents' values or standards for her, except in one important matter. Although her parents were paying for college for her older brother, they had simply assumed that she would become a secretary until she married. College, they made clear, did not seem to be a good investment for a girl. But Andrea, quietly and simply, declared that she would put herself through college, went out and found a part-time job in an office, and enrolled in a public, inexpensive university. She expressed no sense of rebellion or resentment about her parents' attitude. She was simply doing what she wanted to do.

At college, however, she met many people with views and experiences different from her parents'. It was a shock to be in a secular world. Eventually, she came to realize that the bedrock assumptions of her family and religion were "not necessarily the only right way to be," and this realization led to some battles at home to force her parents to loosen their control. Her mother was hesitant about some of her new college friends and did not like Andrea going out with people she did not know well.

Andrea was interested in the varieties of her new friends' ways of thinking; she seemed to be in search of a vehicle by which to achieve independence from her parents. It came in the form of a man with whom she developed a serious relationship in her sophomore year. Arnold seemed to be a lot like her but more self-assured. He was supportive of her ambitions and desire for education and consoled and encouraged her when she felt pressured or worried about her future. "He made me more sure of myself, more self-confident and willing to try new things. It was important just having someone there who thought a lot of me. He helped me to grow up." Her relationship with Arnold made it possible for Andrea to clearly define herself as different from her parents; the potential loss of their love was replaced by his. She and Arnold planned to marry after their graduation and support themselves through medical school. Andrea was eager to move away from her parents, to begin what seemed to be a promising life with Arnold.

Throughout her growing-up years, especially throughout college, Andrea showed a pattern of complex and varied identifications with many people. Teachers, in particular, were influential in helping her choose to pursue her interest in medicine. In addition, she enjoyed listening intently to her friends, sought out new people, and thought about the differences between herself and others. She had always emulated strong, decisive people.

Although she had once viewed her father as strong and active, she had come to feel that he was under her mother's control, and she felt that an important part of her commitment to her fiancé was that he differed from her father in this respect. Andrea showed a range of feeling in regard to each of her parents, admiring some of their characteristics, resenting others. At the same time that she loved them, she got angry at them for overprotecting her. Her parents, then, were not wholly gratifying—at least by the time she reached adolescence. Her mother seemed too restrictive and her father too passive to intervene for her against her mother's control. Through her relationship with Arnold, she was able to give up her dependence on them without simply substituting him for them and without having to untie completely her emotional bonds to them. With his support, she could move forward. This need for support was the theme of a recurrent childhood daydream she reported: "I used to daydream about a castle out in the woods with dungeons. It was spooky, but exciting, with things there trying to attack me. But I was looking for the treasure. I was with a friend, and as long as someone is with me, I don't get scared."

Andrea laughed nervously throughout the college interview and seemed to be almost devoid of insight. Her blandness gave her an absence of charm. She described people in her life in distant ways, and most of her interests centered on solitary activities. The clinical team thought her someone who had difficulty being close to others or even aware of her own needs and emotions. However, the details of Andrea's life evidenced her fortitude and persistence. She appeared to be a woman with a goal, a goal of her own choosing, a goal she was pursuing without looking right or left or letting other things distract her.

Andrea at Thirty-Four. Experience was kind to Andrea, and she grew into a much warmer, more relaxed, more open woman than she had been in college. Still definitive and tough-minded, she did some thinking about herself that she could not do in college and, in general, has become softer and less brittle.

At age thirty-four, Andrea has just finished medical training and also an advanced degree in biochemistry. She is planning to practice part-time and to do research part-time. She changed her career plans when she developed a special interest in hormonal disorders during her residency in medicine.

Andrea has given up church attendance except while visiting her mother. She feels that religion "lacks applicability" to her present life and that her feelings toward her religion changed when she broke away from the influences of home. Politically, Andrea considers herself to be a liberal, although she says she has become more elitist and more conservative than she was in college.

Her views about sex have also changed in recent years. Now she believes that neither premarital nor extramarital sex is wrong, that the limiting factor is how it affects the relationship with one's partner.

As an adult woman, then, Andrea is still clearly an Identity Achievement. Her commitments have refined, broadened, changed with experience, but they are commitments based on an internalized set of values.

Andrea's life since college has been dominated by her challenging training and her relationship with Arnold, now her husband. The most recent critical decision she had to make was whether to accept an attractive job offer in another city. Because her husband also practices in Philadelphia, where they live, they discussed the relative merits of a commuter marriage and decided against it. Andrea was somewhat disappointed to take a less interesting job but feels that this decision was best. She finds enormous satisfaction in her work, both in helping patients and in her research.

Andrea has had two strong professional role models—one male, one female. She described her woman mentor as "independent. She enjoys life despite problems. She is hard working, and she demonstrates that you can have your own set of values and goals, which may not necessarily correlate with those of others. She also proved to me that it's quite possible to work hard and still enjoy oneself without feeling guilty." These are qualities that Andrea strives to attain. Her male role model is combining the careers she is interested in pursuing and has helped her to figure out how to do that.

Andrea and Arnold married, as planned, just after college graduation. Of her decision to marry, she says, "We thought we were compatible, we loved each other, enjoyed doing things together. He is independent enough and self-confident enough to be able to cope with being married to a professional woman and not feel threatened." She feels that they have had a successful twelve-year marriage, still like doing things together, and enjoy each other's company. They each work hard and support each other's professional activities, even though it is often difficult to take vacations. Andrea feels that they have both grown and changed, but remain compatible, good friends as well as lovers. She seemed happily surprised at how well the relationship has progressed.

Theirs has been a somewhat nontraditional marriage, however, in that Andrea has had two intermittent but intense affairs with colleagues. Her husband is aware of these affairs, dislikes them, but understands Andrea's independence and need not to be controlled. These relationships have not threatened the marriage and seem to reflect, for Andrea, her need to define her life in her own way. Andrea has a strikingly objective attitude about her marriage and experiences no need to idealize it. Arnold had been somewhat resentful of the long hours she spent at the hospital during residency, and she resented his resentment. When she then decided to enroll in a doctoral program, necessitating more long hours, he told her that he might not be there when she finished. Andrea, commenting on her stubbornness, felt that it was a chance she would have to take. Andrea regards Arnold as less career oriented than she and the more needy partner in the relationship. She often likes to do independent things with friends, and he has a hard time finding other companionship. But she feels a special intimacy with him that she has felt with no one else in her life. "We have deep feeling and a long history together, and so far he's always won over anyone else."

Accustomed to a fast-paced life with much freedom, Andrea and Arnold have decided not to have children. "When I'd think about it, I'd think that having children was not something I want to do now. Gradually I realized that I'm not going to be able to do everything. I didn't think I could take care of them and maintain my life-style and my work." She does not want to devote the time necessary to raising them, and her husband is of similar mind. She values her independence and spontaneity, and wants to give attention to her career. "I do not feel the need to procreate," she said.

Her decision not to have children is not surprising, even in light of her highly traditional family background, in that Andrea has repeatedly been a pathfinder, setting her own goals and resisting the crowd. From the time she was the somewhat isolated "bookworm" of junior high, she has learned to rely on her inner resources, to decide and then to act. Her parents expected her to go to secretarial school, consistent with their views of a woman's appropriate aspirations, so Andrea paid her own way through school. Frequently, during her training, she has held out against group pressures and insisted on doing what she thought was right. Similarly, her combination of careers has been an unusual one, as is the research problem she has tackled. The adventurousness and the inner strength, resting as it does on an important relationship with one necessary, loving, supportive other, have been constants in Andrea's life.

Andrea's father died six years ago, and she discussed his death mainly as it influenced her mother. Her mother is constantly critical of Andrea's life-style and choice of husband, but she has set clear limits for her mother, and they remain affectionate and on good terms. "I tell her what I think she won't get upset about. She realizes that, at this point, if she pushes me too much, she won't see me." Although she does not particularly enjoy the time spent with her mother, she carries out her daughterly duty with genuine care. She and her mother have little that they deeply share, but she tries to find some things to do with her mother that will bring them both pleasure.

Andrea feels that she is much like her family in being concerned about others, but her family was much more traditional about women's roles and about morals than she is. Andrea also tends to value friendships more than her family did and sees friends as substituting for an extended family. She tends, however, to have more friendships with males because she has more in common with them than with women and has only recently found women who are enough like her for friendships to form.

For Andrea, the sense of freedom is critically important. She returns again and again to the idea of her life-style as the most valued part of her life, the feeling that she is free to do what she wants when she wants to. When not working, she enjoys cooking, reading, and taking long bicycle tours. She relishes being able to express her interests, to experience life.

Despite the extraordinary amount of time and investment she has made in her career, Andrea does not put her career at the center of herself. "I consider that the bond with other people is most important; career is low in the microcosm. My husband, other friends, how I'm interrelating—that's what matters most. Feeling close to someone, being able to talk to and understand someone, having people you feel comfortable with, who have a similar outlook on life—that's what matters most. The worst feeling would be to be completely alone, to have no one to talk to."

About the future, Andrea anticipates change. She cannot predict research funding, and changes in funding may necessitate a move. So far, no other man has seriously competed with her husband for her affections, but she cannot be certain that no one ever will. As she imagines change, she does so with a glint in her eye, another adventure before her. Although she values those things and people that are integral parts of her life, she is moving forward, seeing what else there may be.

From an early age, Andrea appeared to have separated herself from her mother's control. She turned to her father, who supported and encouraged her, although he was available only distantly and infrequently. Whatever psychological process made it possible, Andrea is not emotionally needy and can manage to be alone. She is a reality-oriented woman, stays goal directed, does not revel in her inner world. She recognizes the risks in making decisions but makes them nevertheless, feeling that if they do not work out, she can make other ones. The closest she comes to inner conflict is over her interests in men other than her husband. But of these interests she says simply, "It's something I feel I need" and has managed to find a niche for this need in the structure of her life.

Andrea, then, is the pathfinder among the Identity Achievements and has attained the most career success in terms of prestige and difficulty. She has also been the most daring in her relationships, does not refrain from defining relationships in her own terms. From her decision to attend college in high school to her decision to forgo children, Andrea has used her inner resources to make her life conform to her. But she has done this simply and quietly, without Sturm und Drang.

It is also possible to achieve identity without dramatic adolescent struggles, without forging new paths, and without moving far from home at all. A young woman may well allow herself to deeply notice alternative ways of being and yet to freely choose the values and paths that have been hers all along. Such choice is not based on the reflexive sense of necessity that typifies the Foreclosures. Rather, it is a thoughtful choice, an opting for what seems to be of value in what was prologue to the choice. With the Identity Achievements such as these, however, the distance from the Foreclosure position seems shorter, as will be evident in Amanda.

Amanda

Amanda in College. Amanda was majoring in psychology in college, hoping to work with retarded children. Although her parents had hoped she would go to college, they did not encourage any particular career direction. Amanda was not engaged by her studies, found that the learning was too pressured, and looked forward to getting out of school and working. She had been active as a Catholic when younger, raised in a close Italian family. Toward the end of high school, she began to doubt her religious beliefs, finding some of the rules of the church "ridiculous" and finding the people in her church bigoted and narrow-minded. In breaking with her church, in taking a position for birth control, Amanda staked her difference from her family and was on the way to Identity Achievement.

For six years, spanning high school and college, Amanda was seriously involved with a black man, much to the dismay of her strict and traditional family. She did not see this relationship as an aspect of rebellion at the time and expected her family and friends to accept him. "That was a decision I had to make. With religion talking about love thy neighbor and all men are equal, and it was all right until he asked me out. Now, after six years, my family has accepted it." She intended to marry this man. "It's a decision I've thought about for a long time, and it still bothers me. But when I think about it, I know it's going to be my life, and I can't go against my own ideas for my parents."

While in college, Amanda spoke with great warmth about her family. They were close, had a lot of family traditions. They were always there for financial and emotional support, but there was no privacy. Everyone always knew everything you were doing. Her father had been a strict disciplinarian, and she battled him about rules and going out; she felt she did not get along well with him. Amanda saw her mother as "very giving— always a lot of emotional support. She'd give anything to her family, and she's very attached to her family." In looking back, she saw her family as "almost ideal," except she felt that her mother was too submissive to her father, always giving in to him. She hoped she could be less submissive than her mother, which she was on the way to becoming.

Amanda grew up in the enclave of a large extended family. "It was like having ten mothers." There were many cousins as well as many friends. Popular in high school, she was a cheerleader and on student council. Amanda's adolescence was rooted and secure. As she spoke of her college years, Amanda stressed the interpersonal learning that she had had to do. She learned about her limitations in a volunteer job she had. "Experience has taught me not to be so idealistic. When I went into the treatment center for retarded children, I thought that if I just cared enough, it would change things. That a lot of these people just never had anyone that really cared, and I did really care; and in a lot of cases things didn't work out, and I didn't become callous, but it's taught me that there are a lot of limitations working within certain structures. You want to do so much, yet you can't." Fortunately, Amanda had a supportive supervisor who "showed me the realities of various situations and encouraged me to go to graduate school." This man helped her to maintain her goals despite frustration.

As she finished college, Amanda was hoping to go to graduate school, to work for awhile before having children and then again after they were school age. She was optimistic about the future, expanding her sensibilities, eager to see how the world really was.

Amanda in college had a vibrant, emotionally expressive quality. She had thought deeply about herself and other people, was preparing herself to fight the prejudice her anticipated marriage would evoke from strangers, and was also intent on exploring the world of both work and people. That she remained fiercely loving of her family did not interfere with her ambition. She had achieved a sense of individuality without undoing emotional ties.

Amanda at Thirty-Three. At age thirty-three, Amanda was less vivacious and energetic and had gained fifty pounds. Life's burdens were greater than she had expected, and her life has taken significantly different directions than she had planned. She looked very maternal as she sat in her nursing office, and maternal is what her life has come to be about.

Shortly after college, Amanda's relationship with her long-term boyfriend began to unravel as he became less reliable, more involved in drugs, less committed to pursuing his education. When he said that he was no longer interested in marriage and children, Amanda angrily but reluctantly ended the relationship to "see what else was out there." She turned to a colleague she had known for some years. They had similar values. This relationship with George was less intense emotionally, less filled with ups and downs, but they "fit together" well and married within a year. She found George to be "sensitive, caring, same values, handsome, somewhat shy, responsible, and loved children."

From the time she became involved with George, Amanda's work goals became secondary. "Family and children were very important to both of us." At the same time, her experiences in the state school for retarded children where she taught were becoming increasingly disappointing. She was burning out on the paperwork and bureaucracy and eventually enrolled in a nursing program because she saw nursing as offering flexibility for a working mother.

Amanda had her first child three years after her marriage, did not work for four years while she pursued evening classes in nursing. Financial necessity drove her back to work after the birth of a second child, but she has arranged her working hours so that the children are in daycare as little as possible. As a result, she works many evening and night shifts. Still traditional about family roles, she does all the cooking and housework as well.

Amanda's main focus in life is spending time with her children. "I believe they need quantity and quality of time with both parents." She wistfully regrets that physical problems have prevented her from having more children. The children are also George's main interest. They have little time alone together, but she feels that when the children are grown and gone, they will have time enough to be alone.

If she could afford it, Amanda would not work at all. She wishes for more time with her children and time for crafts and exercise. But she does say, "I love the people I work with. We're a small, closely knit team." And Amanda is proud that she is the first woman in her extended family to both work and raise children. In that sense, she sees herself as a pathfinder.

Still close to her extended family, who live in a neighbor-

ing town, Amanda rather savors her role as the one who is a little different. She had to do lots of justifying to her family, especially for buying a large, pretty house, which has made her work
necessary. She has the continual feeling that "a big group is
watching me, asking in subtle, indirect ways if I am sure I am
doing the right thing." A great joy to Amanda was overhearing
her mother describing her to someone else: "Amanda's happily
married and her kids are OK." With great relief, Amanda felt
she had achieved her mother's blessing.

Amanda wants her children to grow up the way she did,
with a warm, loving extended family, with a sense of community. To this end, she has decided to raise them Catholic, as she
was raised. "I always thought God was a good and kind and caring person. I want them to get a sense of humanity, not the details of religion." As a mother, Amanda feels that she is more
open with her children and shelters them less than her parents
did her.

Given the traditionalism of her family, Amanda has psychologically moved some distance from home. At the same
time, she founds her life on their fundamental values. The return to their values has led to a new, harmonious relationship
with her father, who can now love her children and approve of
her. "I was always his good little girl, his shining star as far as
education was concerned." But nothing has won his approval as
much as her husband and children. Amanda has remained close
to her mother, who is still the first person she turns to in a
crisis. She knows her mother is behind her, whatever she does.

Amanda, then, has chosen a route much like her mother's
but she chose it on her own terms, knowing that she might have
chosen otherwise. As she looks back, she wonders if her black
boyfriend might have represented some sort of rebellion but
then dismisses this as an unimportant question. Whether she
made her choice out of fear or out of the discovery of what was
fundamentally important to her is a question that neither she
nor I can answer. In that episode of her life, she proved to herself that she could choose, which helped her to firm her sense of
individuality. She had most wanted to become a giving, helping
person and discovered that she could do that most meaningfully

with her own children. She continues to think through her choices rather than automatically doing what is expected of her. Amanda sees herself as breaking new ground, showing her family that she can amalgamate the cherished family-centered values with a professional life and an upwardly mobile life-style. In this adventure, she takes pride.

Identity Achievements as a Group

The central theme that distinguishes the Identity Achievements from the other groups, both at adolescence and adulthood, is that of independence. Independence, however, is a complex and somewhat misleading word. The danger is that it conjures up notions of the lone frontiersman, who forges a path unconnected to others. This is not the form of independence to be found among the Identity Achievements.

The adolescence of the Identity Achievements is typically a struggle to wrest free a part of the personality so that it is available for exploration, for choice, and for flexible recombination of elements into a highly personal identity. This struggle does not occur among the Foreclosures, who bypass this developmental work in favor of carrying forward childhood-based solutions. Independence, then, involves a renunciation of some of the narcissistic gratifications of childhood, a liberation from those ties so that new ties may be formed.

This developmental work is, most importantly, an internal liberation. It is not always readily observable or easily connected to behaviors. If we look closely at the adolescence of Alice and Andrea, we observe two major paths through adolescence to be found among the Identity Achievements, paths that lead to the sort of independence necessary for identity formation. (Amanda's history of identity formation rests somewhere between these paths.) Alice exemplifies a road to identity formation close to the one outlined by Erikson, who stresses the experience of the Moratorium phase. She underwent a clear and visible period of uncertainty as a late adolescent, a time of testing and trial followed by a period of decision. She cut her ties to home, tried drugs and sex, and experimented with various kinds of relationships. As she put it she "went wild" for a time. For Andrea, the process was less overt. Her middle-adolescent development followed a somewhat characteristic Foreclosure pattern, and although her postcrisis identity was formulated on her own terms, she was, at the end of adolescence, less individuated than Alice. She was becoming a differentiated person through Arnold but had not yet found the means to express this new self. By the end of college, Alice had moved further from her earlier adolescent self than had Andrea and seemed to be headed in a more creative direction. In adulthood, however, Andrea is forging the unique path, more clearly her own self. Amanda falls somewhere between these two patterns, staking her independence as an adolescent, somewhat noisily, on a forbidden relationship. Once her right to independence was acknowledged, once she realized she could do what she wanted to, she felt free to choose not to.

Without question, the dynamics of adolescence, reflecting as they do personality configurations based in early childhood, are critical to the first important life-course decisions. It is therefore important to observe carefully the internal configurations in these Identity Achievement women as they appeared as adolescents and to contrast them with the inner situation of the Foreclosures.

Andrea, as a college freshman, was not terribly different from the Foreclosures in outlook. Like the Foreclosures, she had a history of peer rejection and somewhat overprotective and overinvolved parents. Unlike the Foreclosures, however, she did not retreat from the rejection. Instead, she turned to her own capacities and efforts for self-esteem, confident that she could derive self-esteem through her own actions and her effect on the world. Andrea had also integrated her basic trust in and love for her parents with a realistic appraisal of them. She was able to experience ambivalence toward them, unlike the Foreclosures' idealization of their parents. She could view each parent as having something to offer her, could identify in part with each of them without having to buy the whole package. In this sense, she was, by the end of college, individuated from her parents, could experience each of them as distinct and separate human beings. What this developmental course presaged for Andrea, and for others in this group like her, was the capacity, at the right time and under the right set of circumstances, to renounce the self-esteem derived from pleasing parents and to struggle for maturity. For Andrea and others like her, maturity came gradually rather than in identifiable and intense conflict. The testing of identity possibilities was largely silent and internal.

Alice and other women in this group like her seem to have had parents whom they could not please enough. Alice's parents were strict, they structured her but did not provide enough emotional nourishment. Her first line of defense, at the age of twelve, was to choose someone to substitute for these unpleaseable parents, someone who would structure her life for her and allow her to succeed at being good. Her decision to leave home and her boyfriend and to go to college was a reflection, however, of her confidence in her own abilities, which led her, by surprise, to cut her ties to her boyfriend and to her hometown. Like Andrea, Alice had learned to derive self-esteem both from being loved and from her own competence.

Amanda also learned to value her own skills and abilities, paramount for her in the interpersonal sphere. Although she does not call attention to her skillfulness, she must have had enormous resourcefulness to manage her unusual relationship, to finally win her family's acceptance, to stand up to the prejudice and disfavor she incurred, all without severing her relationships within her family. Amanda internalized a sense of her competence with other people, beyond being loved by them.

It is important to emphasize at this point that the Identity Achievements are no higher in intelligence or talent than any of the other groups. They differ in their valuation of their own competence and the role they give it in their personality structure. For Identity Achievement women, their capacities to have an effect on the world become a highly important part of their self-definition. Their actions come to produce intrinsic rewards—that is, what matters is not making others proud of them but feeling proud of themselves. They know they can offer something of value to an outside world, sometimes the abstract world and sometimes the personal world, and they take joy in their abilities to make the world respond to them. Stating this task simply, however, obscures how hard a task it is.

As adolescents, Identity Achievements are most likely of all the groups to speak of experiences in which they could be on their own and survive. Or they describe instances where they made decisions contrary to their parents' will and found that, although they felt guilty, they were committed to "having my own life." Such women show extraordinary skill in manipulating the environment to support their nascent independence. Teachers, trips to Europe, and roommates are all employed to produce new modes of experiencing the self, without completely giving up old modes until the new ones are consolidated.

For Identity Achievements the college years are often a highly ambivalent period, especially for those dramatically separating from parents. There is always the possibility of giving up the venture altogether, of failing to make a success of the new identity constellation. The regressive wish to seek the safety of the Foreclosure position is often painfully present. This wish is expressed eloquently in a dream of one of the other Identity Achievements: "I dreamt I was driving down a hill with my father. Then I stopped the car and let him out and kept driving down the hill. Sometimes I would think I would just drive around the block and pick him up again, but I didn't." This dream captures the essence of the separation-individuation process of adolescence. It is important that father be there to be picked up—it is the adolescent who must choose to drive on. And, having not picked up father, the adolescent is bound to feel guilty.

One central aspect of personality functioning among the Identity Achievements during adolescence is the capacity to tolerate guilt. To dare to move past the bounds of childhood evokes in the developing woman some sense of having betrayed her parents. To do something she cannot tell her mother about causes intense pangs of conscience. As in the dream, to grow up is to strand one's father. The Foreclosures will do just about anything to avoid this experience, and, as we will see later, the Moratoriums become overwhelmed by it. But the Identity Achievements seem able to incur guilt in tolerable doses and to learn to live with it. As a result, the Identity Achievements, when interviewed in college, all had an edge of depression and sadness about them. They felt themselves turning their backs, however slightly, on their parents and felt guilty. But they bore the guilt, paid the price in sorrow, and were therefore able to mature. By the time they were thirty-four, their guilt, and the resultant depression, had disappeared.

The most typical pattern for achieving identity during late adolescence is for a young woman to form a relationship with a man who will help her become less dependent on her parents. Unlike the Foreclosures, who choose men as substitute objects of dependence, people who will care for them as their parents did, Identity Achievements choose men who will care about them and replace some of the self-esteem that is inevitably lost as distance from parents increases. What they look for in a man is ego support, someone who will buttress their wishes to do and be in the world, who will anchor and soothe them but will allow them to experience themselves. Andrea, for example, continually returns to the theme of her husband supporting her career, being understanding of her rigorous training, sharing her successes, and lamenting her frustrations. That Andrea's mother is unable to support her in this way—is, indeed, actively opposed to her daughter's life-style—does not matter to her, as it has not since late in college. Similarly, Amanda looks to her husband to support her decision to work while raising children. This support has given her the strength to counter her family's consternation and doubt about her choice.

Here, then, is one of the paradoxes of the Identity Achievement women's "independence." Their independence, in effect, seems to rest on the support of a man (or, in the case of the two unmarried Achievements, on important friends) for their right to take pride in their own accomplishments. All the married Achievement women in this group mentioned their husbands' support of their work-related efforts as important. By contrast, no Foreclosure woman mentioned such support. Work clearly has different meanings to the women in the two groups, reflecting the different place it has in their identities.

Work, in early adulthood, is the fulfillment of the identity strands opened in late adolescence for self-esteem. As a result, Identity Achievement women are likely to be more demanding of their work than are Foreclosure women. For Foreclosure women, work is a means of continuing to meet others' expectations, and they are highly successful and valued employees. They work hard for rewards, are likely to be promoted, and they evaluate their work efforts by whether others are pleased with them. Identity Achievement women, by contrast, expect that their work will allow them to experience their capacity to have an effect on the world. They are less needy of external rewards and can be dissatisfied with work even if their superiors are pleased with them, even if they are succeeding. For Alice, for example, moving up in the hierarchy, getting promoted to more responsible positions, led to her dissatisfaction with her work. When she could be directly helpful to others, she found joy in her efforts; battling a bureaucracy, despite her prestigious title, held no appeal for her.

Identity Achievements are the most likely of the groups to have changed professions after a period of time in the jobs they initially chose at the end of college. Of the eight Identity Achievements, seven are now in different occupations than they had chosen in college in contrast to none of the eight Foreclosures. One Identity Achievement felt forced to revise her career plans when she was unable to realize her hopes to work in the foreign service. Most of the others made career changes because of disillusionment with the bureaucratic structures they found themselves in. Aware that they could not reach their goals within the systems available to them, these women suffered new crisis periods in which they reevaluated their goals. Most of these women, using their own experiences, then set out to make more realistic choices and retrained on the basis of their now more mature conception of how work is done in the world. Alice retrained for speech therapy, a more independent profession than physical therapy, when work within an institutional framework became unfulfilling. Andrea worked out a unique career that did not follow the typical medical route. Amanda became dissatisfied with a bureaucracy that interfered with her idealistic wishes to help children and decided to invest herself in raising her own. Another Identity Achievement woman, who began a teaching career but found she disliked the snobbism of teenagers, decided to promote her amateur interest in photography to a full-time vocation. Yet another decided, in the midst of a successful but frustrating teaching career, to explore opportunities in business.

Because part of the definition of Identity Achievement status at the end of college was commitment to aspects of psychosocial identity, including occupation, one might well question the depth of that commitment in light of the fact that so many make later changes. Yet to say that these commitments lacked depth would be fallacious and would overlook the subtle yet reliable basis of women's identity formation. Other research, including research based on these subjects, has repeatedly shown that for women occupational identity is less predictive of overall identity status than is ideological and interpersonal identity (Schenkel and Marcia, 1972; Bilsker, Schiedel, and Marcia, 1987). For women, commitment to aspects of the self in relation to others as well as to belief systems forms the nucleus of the identity constellation. In a sense, occupational identity grows out of that nucleus. Once a woman has committed herself to whom she wants to be in relation to others, how she wants to contribute to others, her occupational identity becomes a means of expressing aspects of this basic sense of self. With identity related to but not rooted in career goals, Identity Achievement women are flexible about their jobs and, into their early thirties, are still considering options.

These career changes among the Identity Achievements are the result of thought and reflection rather than impulse. They are an expression of the wish that work provide something for them. The capacity to integrate identity, wrought in the stress of liberation from parental expectations and values, leads them to be able to repeat this integration process during adulthood. The Identity Achievement women seem, for the most part, not wedded to "being" a certain occupation. Amanda, for example, shifted from teaching to nursing because the hours were more flexible, and nursing seemed more easily combined with being a mother. Another, once she married, was freed from

the necessity of supporting herself financially, which made possible her decision to pursue seriously her interest in photography.

For most of the Identity Achievement women then, work
is something to do rather than something to be. As these wom-
en talk about their work, it often has little more weight in their
overall identity than does their interest in a certain sport or
craft. Jogging can feel as much a part of their identity as can
doing physical therapy. More realistic and more discouraged
about the gratifications of the work world when first embark-
ing on their careers, these women are likely to say that they
long most for time to pursue an interest in pottery or book-
binding or travel.

Just as these women do not define themselves by their
work, they also do not define themselves as mother of someone
or wife of someone. The hallmark of the Identity Achievement
is the balance among work, relationships, and interests. All of
the Achievements have made relationship primary in their lives.
Two women, who married somewhat unusual men, have shaped
their lives within the bounds provided by the husbands' careers.
One woman, for example, married a man in the foreign service
and has tempered and tailored her career interests to the necessity of moving to a new country every few years. She retrained
as a nurse, with the thought that there would be need for nurses
wherever they live. Although she has been somewhat frustrated
in her professional pursuits, she satisfies her need for achievement through hobbies and through devoted and careful mothering of their children.

For the Achievements, success in relationship still comes
first. When Alice's first marriage was crumbling, she was able to
seek some refuge in her successful career but did not feel fully
realized as a person until she was able to work in the context of a
healthy relationship. Identity Achievements tend to create marriages that are partnerships, an outcome of consideration of
both individuals' needs. They are less bound to traditional concepts of marriage than Foreclosures; they are likely to structure
relationships based on the needs of the partners rather than on
ideas of how marriage is supposed to be.

The need to combine self-in-the-world and self-in-relation

appears to be a deep and early aspect of Identity Achievement women. Previous research on the early memories of this group shows that Identity Achievements have a typical and unique pattern (Josselson, 1982). Early memories are assumed to reflect personal myths at the core of the sense of self. These memories represent the experience of the self in the past as it is experienced in the present and are therefore a reflection of central aspects of identity structure.

Early memories collected from these women at the end of adolescence show that Identity Achievements are more likely than other groups to have memories in which they blend and integrate aspects of both security and adventurousness. Where the early memories of Foreclosure women tend to reflect their preoccupation with themes of basic security and dependence, the memories of Identity Achievement women integrate their needs both for relatedness and for self-assertion (see also Orlofsky and Frank, 1986). They "do," but in the context of a secure relationship, drawing on the relationship as a wellspring for their efforts. In a sense, Andrea, in her dream, stated the central dynamic of the Achievements: "As long as someone is with me, I don't get scared." She can venture, can attempt to realize her potential, as long as she has someone beside her.

What the Identity Achievements have achieved, then, is the capacity to forge identity, irrespective of its content. The Identity Achievement group is capable of great shifts in the expression of their identity—they are flexible. Yet they are flexible within a context of continuity. These women can commit themselves sequentially to varieties of activities, including work, but they are committed to how they want to experience the world and to the values they wish to realize in action.

Whereas for the adult Foreclosures security remains the predominant issue, the key word for the Identity Achievements during early adulthood is self-confidence. When these women speak of their experiences, they emphasize the confidence in themselves that was gained or lost and how they learned about what they were capable of. The struggle for independence in adolescence, then, seems to be the progenitor of the struggle for self-confidence in early adulthood. Relinquishing the reassuring ties to internalized parents and the concomitant self-esteem that derives from being a good girl for good parents forces the Identity Achievement woman to test out her own capacities and form evaluations of the self based on experience rather than love.

Identity Achievement women are, for the most part, not highly introspective or self-reflective. Like the Foreclosures, they are mainly goal oriented. They tend not to feast on ambivalence or wallow in feeling. They seem to take themselves at face value and to deny or suppress internal conflict. In this sense, they are reminiscent of the Harvard men Vaillant (1977) studied, among whom the most psychologically healthy were those who utilized defenses of suppression and altruism. Vaillant suggests that the most mature defenses are doing for others and containing disruptive emotion, and these are the defenses Identity Achievements use most.

Yet the Identity Achievements, in contrast to the Foreclosures, are philosophical about their lives. They have spent much of their twenties learning what they can and cannot control and learning to maintain self-esteem in the face of the uncontrollable. Looking at their lives from age thirty-four, nearly all the Achievements see their circumstances as a combination of luck and hard work. "Luck," as one put it, "keeps disaster away." They see themselves as lucky to have been born with talent or beauty. Luck provides opportunities for skill and hard work. Andrea said, "I consider myself lucky. I don't think anyone is completely in control of their own destiny. I've worked hard to put myself in the position to be considered for positions, but I feel luck played an important part in my career."

This statement stands in contrast to the Foreclosure reflections on the same matters. More than half the Foreclosures flatly denied that luck had anything to do with their success or accomplishment. "I'm in charge of my luck," said one. "I have made the important decisions," said another. This Foreclosure need for certainty and control does not appear among the Identity Achievements. Mature identity formation among women seems to involve a tolerance for ambiguity, a resignation to what is outside one's control, as well as increasing confidence in the capacity to affect what can be controlled.

If the achievement of the Identity Achievements is the capacity to forge identity, we can well imagine that these women's lives will continue to change. We see among these thirty-four-year-olds lives that work for this developmental period but lives in which important needs and wishes lie dormant, awaiting a new era for their realization. Although not dissatisfied with their lives, the Identity Achievements remain focused toward the future, anticipating the new experiences they will have, certain that they will greet new adventures with a flexible sense of self. These women will differentiate further and explore other aspects of themselves. They have not yet finished with becoming.

Chapter 6

Daughters of Crisis: The Moratoriums

> Do I dare
> Disturb the universe?
> In a minute there is time
> For decisions and revisions which a minute will re-
> verse.
> —*T. S. Eliot,* "The Love Song of J. Alfred Prufrock"

The women we shall meet in this chapter capture in reality the widespread conception of what adolescence is all about. In this group are the women who left their churches, marched in antiwar protests, became feminists, criticized their parents, experimented with sex—and felt guilty. The Moratorium women seemed to have the acuity of vision, the responsiveness to social problems, and the psychological closeness to great philosophical questions so often sentimentalized by observers of youth. They were, above all, aware of choice and often paralyzed by their awareness. Emotionally attuned to options, these women knew that they could design their own lives but frequently wanted to choose both sides of a contradiction. They dreamt of glorious careers helping others but were unsure how to translate this dream into realistic occupational choice. They were tempted and intrigued by sexual experience but were not yet fully ready to give up the comforts of being virginal girls.

The Moratorium phase is one of testing and searching for new identities. Here is where daring to do something different and taking a risk on the unknown come into play. Women who were in such a phase in college were, without question, the most interesting, lively, and engaging women who took part in this study. They struggled with the great questions of life and told their stories in the most sensitive and insightful ways. Some experienced torrents of feeling so intense that it was frequently heart-rending to listen to them.

Despite their evident charm, the persistent and puzzling finding, throughout all research (Marcia, 1980) on the identity statuses, has been that female Moratoriums do not show the positive, adaptive personality characteristics of their male counterparts. Although male Moratoriums behave much like Identity Achievements on personality measures, female Moratoriums behave much like Diffusions. In particular, they show lower self-esteem and greater anxiety than do Identity Achievements and Foreclosures. Many writers in this area have speculated that perhaps the Moratorium phase is less healthy and desirable for women than for men (recall that it is the female Foreclosures who resemble Identity Achievements). Perhaps our society does not encourage or support a Moratorium phase for women, valuing commitment above exploration (see Marcia, 1980).

Two research papers have presented data that suggest that although female Moratoriums may superficially be more like Diffusions, they may more deeply have greater psychological strength that lies nascent, not ready to be put to use (Ginsburg and Orlofsky, 1981; Josselson, 1982). If that is true, then the Moratorium phase is an upsetting one for women but not indicative of long-term difficulty. Only with the longitudinal data of this study can we answer the question of what becomes of Moratoriums: How do they finally choose? And how do they live with their choices?

Ten women who had been classified as Moratoriums in college participated in the follow-up study. For many, their current identity status was hard to classify. Because of the way the identity statuses were constructed and defined, a woman who had undergone a period of testing and exploration could then be classified only as Identity Achievement, Diffusion, or still Moratorium. The theory did not take into account a phenomenon that I was unprepared for: Some of the Moratorium women went back to being Foreclosures.* To follow the letter of the rules of identity-status categorizing, I would be required to rate such women as Identity Achievements. After all, they had undergone a crisis and then made commitments, even if the commitment was to drop down the developmental ladder back to older, safer patterns. I decided, therefore, to create a new category for adult women, Foreclosure/Achievement, to distinguish them from the true Identity Achievements, who made commitments on their own, not someone else's, terms.

Meeting the Moratorium group ten to twelve years later, I found seven married, one divorced, and two single. Only two had children by age thirty-four. Three of the ten former Moratoriums have gone on to resolve the crisis state with clearly defined, individually determined identities. One was still struggling to decide what to commit herself to. The remaining six were somewhere on the Foreclosure/Achievement continuum, having made commitments, but having more or less returned to old values and life patterns, more or less based on willful choice.

Millie

Millie in College. Millie was a perky, cherubic-looking young woman who came to the interview dressed in the "hippie" garb that came to symbolize the era of the late 1960s and early 1970s. Millie was raised in a New York suburb, the middle of three children. Neither of her parents had attended college, but they wanted her to have as much education as possible. She ventured away from home to a large, private university in Philadelphia.

---

*Marcia (1976) encountered the same phenomenon in his follow-up study of men. He suggested that these were perhaps people who had been doing some decision making around the time of the college-age interview but who had never seriously departed from Foreclosure identities.

Millie had expected that she would become a nurse like her mother but found that she did not "have the temperament." Since then, she had switched her major three times. After giving up on nursing, she applied for a physical therapy program but was not accepted because of her grades; so she opted for a psychology major. Psychology, she found, was making her "get too much into myself," and she was afraid that more psychology would "screw me up," so she changed again to biology. This change made sense to her because she had begun to think about doing cancer research as a result of two summers she had spent working in a nursing home. Having developed a close relationship with one particular dying woman, she became quite upset about the ravages of cancer and thought that she might like to take part in searching for a cure. After a few semesters of biology courses, however, Millie was becoming upset at the idea of killing frogs in her physiology class and had come to realize that she would not have the stomach to do cancer research. She wished she had just gone into teaching, but it was too late. Of her future occupation, she said, "I think I'd like to be a bum. I've felt really tied down by school, and I'd like to start doing some traveling. I don't want to settle down in a job right now since I've been settled down in school for so long. I feel like I've missed a lot, and I'd like to just get a job like a waitress and just travel around and meet people and be exposed to things. I'd like to learn a little about life before I settle down into a routine."

Millie was not sure about the prospect of marriage, but she said that she figured she would probably marry eventually. "I don't like to think of myself as forty years old and unmarried, but right now I can't imagine it. I can imagine loving someone or living with someone, but as soon as there is a legal bond —that this is the way it's going to be—I get scared." As for children, she said, "I don't want my life to be my children. I want my own life. I've seen too many parents—like mine—who have put their whole lives into their children, and then when the children grow up, they're lost. You've got to realize from the start that eventually they're going to leave."

Raised in the strictest Catholic tradition, she had become increasingly aware of the church's "hypocrisy." When she noticed that many people were going to church only to see what other people were wearing, she stopped going to church. "I know my parents would like me to go to church, and I'd like to do it for them, but I couldn't because I'd be a hypocrite, and I'd be deceiving them into thinking I'm a good Catholic girl again when I'm not." But she was not sure what to believe instead. "I do want to believe," she said, "because just to believe in reality is not so nice because there are a lot of things in reality that are not so nice." She tried to develop a personal ethical system but became stymied when she thought about how she might raise children. "I went to Catholic schools, and those things are ingrained in me. I can cut down the Catholic Church, but when I hear someone else do it, I get really defensive."

Millie had had intense political struggles in regard to involvement in antiwar protests. "I was believing what people were saying—that you can give up your grades for people who are over in Viet Nam dying. You can make a sacrifice for them, and I felt, 'Yeah, that's what I'm going to do." But there's no correlation between me not going to class [during the student strike] and them dying over there. It's not doing them any good. And I really got screwed. And nothing came of it. The summer came and everyone went home, and that was it. And I had three incompletes. I'm apathetic now. I really did get involved, and all I could see was I was getting screwed and nothing was coming of it. I don't know what I'd do now. Things aren't the way I'd like them to be in my ideal society."

On the question of premarital sex, Millie had definite views. In her opinion, "someone who is twenty-two and a virgin is perverted." In formulating her own standards, she felt that "you shouldn't make love just to satisfy your animal desires." The first time she had intercourse, it was with a man she loved and hoped to marry. "He changed my ideas because I used to be so inhibited. He changed my whole way of life because I used to be very super straight and closed-minded." She defined her new sexual values based on what she "feels for a person" but worried that "there are a lot of guys who can't handle a sexual relationship and will just think that the girl's a slut." She had gotten over the idea "that if you have sex before you're married, you go straight to hell," but confided that her parents would "freak out" if they knew about her sexual behavior.

Approaching college graduation, Millie remained in a highly conflicted Moratorium state. Uncertain about occupation, religion, politics, or sexual standards, Millie exemplified a pure Moratorium. She had made no commitments in any identity-related aspect of her life but was struggling for them through exploration, trial and error, and thought.

Asked to describe herself, Millie began right off talking about her persistent conflict over being a child or an adult. "I don't think I act my age. I think I act like a kid. Maybe it's that I don't act the way I thought I would act at this age. I used to think that when I was age twenty—I don't know—that I'd walk around discussing Plato or something." This feeling that things in the present—especially the way she was—were not what she had hoped for or expected was a continual theme in her reflections on herself. One of her early memories manifested the same feeling of wish for and fear of the privileges of the next stage: "The day before I went to kindergarten, which I was really looking forward to—very apprehensive but very excited about being a 'big girl.' And my mother said I had to get up at 7 A.M., and I began to think twice about it." Even as a child, she remembered wanting the advantages of growing up but fearing the obligations.

Part of this conflict stemmed from Millie's quest to be right about things. She had little to say about her childhood except that she was always a good girl. She remembered her home as a harmonious, secure environment where she was just like her parents, who were like everyone else's parents, and all the other kids were just like her. Success was easy. Her movement into the more complex world of college startled her because there was no longer the ready, ubiquitous social agreement that she was always right. In her words, "It starts when you're little. You think your parents are gods. Then you find out they're only human, but you still believe what they say because they're your parents. . . . The more I learn, the more middle-of-the-road I become, and it's hard that way because I like to have the answers. But it seems like that's the way it's going—that you just can't say that this is right and this is wrong."

Millie described her parents as having been affectionate and generous. She felt that her mother often gave her more than she deserved, and she felt guilty about this largess. "She's a good mother. She makes big meals for me and buys me clothes even if she needs them more than me." Her father, whom she saw as strong, silent, and stable, was the authority at home, and she was frightened of him. He set definite limits for her, and she never felt able to disobey him. The atmosphere at home seemed to have been one of living up to fairly stringent internal and external demands. "I always want to run away, but I never do. My mother once told me that if you shirk responsibility once, you'll just do it all the time, so I never do." But responsibility, especially responsibility for things she had not yet claimed as her own, weighed heavily on Millie.

As a result of these internal and external pressures, Millie always hungered for structure, for something she could bounce against to test whether she were right or wrong. In high school, she became dependent on the boys she dated, trying to live up to what they wanted her to be. Then she got depressed when they broke up with her.

When she first entered college, she felt adrift because of the loss of structure and fell in love with a boy who was to be the focus of her life for the next three years. He was, like her father, a strong, authoritarian figure who set out to mold her and teach her. However, he did so in a sadistic way, poking fun at her middle-class attitudes and beating her occasionally, leaving her frequently. He entertained himself by shocking her with his foul language, his use of drugs, and his increasingly "far out" friends. Millie described him as a "freak," and her parents, after one look at him, despised him. Consequently, Millie became caught in a complex struggle between her parents and her boyfriend, unable to give up her dependence on either of them. "I was torn between my parents and him, and I couldn't condemn them for their motives because they only wanted the best for me; and everything I did was wrong, and everyone was always mad at me; and there I was in the middle." Although she was grateful to her boyfriend for opening her to new ideas and making her less dependent on her parents, she simply shifted her conflicted dependency needs onto him. She idealized him as she had once idealized her parents and tried in every way to gain his approval. Not long before the interview, he had left her once more, this time definitively, and Millie found herself longing for him or, at least, "to be completely in love with someone and to be near people who mean a lot to me." But she had come too far from home to simply return. She was yearning for someone to take the choices away from her and provide the answers. And again she felt a sense of failure because she was never able to fulfill her boyfriend's expectations of her.

As the end of college approached, Millie was dealing with the impending separation from her friends, who were going off in different directions. She was not sure what to do. As she thought about her future, she had to confront the distance she had attained from her past. She said, "I have a different attitude about life. It's strange because the more I think about it, the more confused I get as to what I want to do with myself, where I think I'm going. It's scary in that sense, but it's good in the sense that I'm not just living a life that's already been made for me—like I'm not just falling into a rut that I just didn't even question—that I'd just go to college, get married, live in suburbia, and be a housewife, and naturally I would be a virgin until I got married." Asked how she saw her life five years hence, Millie replied, "I hope I'll have the answers to a lot of questions I'm asking myself now like 'What is life?' and 'What are people?' "

There was cause to worry about Millie at the end of college. Her struggle for individuation seemed to be failing. Instead of being able to dispense with authority and make reality-based decisions, she was engaged in a search for authorities to comply with or rebel against. Although she had managed to disengage from the content of the internalized demands of her childhood, she nevertheless was seeking new goals phrased in the same tone of absoluteness. In trying to grow away from her parents, she unconsciously chose someone who would impose with equivalent force demands opposite to those that her father once imposed on her. Notice, for example, the totalistic statement she made to justify her sexual behavior: Anyone different from her was "perverted."

Millie also felt unable to live up to her own expectations,

unable to be "as big a girl" as she wished. Uncertain of herself and not valuing any of her own capacities or accomplishments, Millie seemed unable to conceive of herself as existing as an individual. Her life seemed centered on how people were reacting to her as she vacillated between pleasing them and shocking them. Her self-esteem derived from the approval of others; there was no sense that she was competent in her own right. Because she did not trust herself and because she feared her own impulses, Millie felt the need for someone to keep her on leash and make her into someone. But, at the same time, her wish to be her own person prevented her from striking the bargain and becoming what someone else wanted her to be.

Millie at Thirty-Four. When I saw Millie at age thirty-four, she was pregnant, relaxed, and talkative. She evinced much less intense conflict and less internal struggle than she had in college. At present, she is focused mainly on her family, her three-year-old daughter and her husband. But she got to this life circumstance by a circuitous route.

In retrospect, from the vantage point of midlife, Millie thinks of herself as having had a goal in college—to do cancer research. Her first job, however, was "terrible." She was in a small lab, with low pay, exposed to asbestos dust. When she complained, they told her she was "a hysterical female," and she quit. Discouraged, she collected unemployment for awhile, then impulsively moved to Florida with a friend. She did odd jobs for money but was living in a rough neighborhood that eventually became so frightening that she abruptly left and returned home to Long Island. She then spent four years as a taxi driver, enjoying the work, the camaraderie, the money, and the freedom.

When she began to tire of taxi driving, she studied to be a paramedical technician, still fascinated by the biological sciences, but then found that the job the course would qualify her for was too demanding and restrictive. "I really don't research things before I do them," she reflected.

Through "luck" she happened on a clerical job in a hospital and found this to be a stimulating world. "I was not working up to my potential in terms of intellect, but it was fascinating."

She stayed there for several years, meanwhile taking computer courses in hopes of increasing her responsibility. But the hospital had no place for her to use these skills, so she took a job in an unrelated agency. Again, she was painfully disappointed in her expectations and found herself in an "oppressive" environment where she did not like the people and had, in fact, little responsibility. This last job crisis was settled when she became pregnant and decided to devote her time to mothering. Since then, she has worked only briefly, as a waitress, for extra money.

Clearly, the issue of her work identity remains a conflicted one for Millie. She misses working, still feels that she wants to make a contribution, to have responsibility and a decent salary. She is still intrigued by medicine but has no idea how she could enter the field and is not willing to take a lot of new courses or expend a lot of effort in training.

Millie still identifies herself as Catholic. She does not feel involved with religion but intends to raise her children as she was raised. "Religion is a good thing to have in times of need— a strength you can draw on." She does not feel that her religious views have changed much in the past ten years, but it is clear from the earlier data that they have. Indeed, she has returned to a position of belief closer to where she was early in adolescence.

The question of politics provokes much anger from Millie. "I think they're all crooks; they lie to get your vote and do whatever they want to anyway." She recalls feeling disillusioned by her political protests in college, and since then has felt that she can have little effect on the political process. "Those people in Washington—they're not going to stand up and notice me." Here again, Millie has the sense that she has not made any difference, that she can have little effect on her world. Millie feels she has become much more conservative than she was in college as a result of seeing how much the government took out of her paycheck, how much waste there is. She became opposed to raising taxes and opposed to welfare. "I used to be idealistic. I used to be naive."

On sexual standards and values, Millie's views are "pretty much the same. Premarital sex is OK. Extramarital sex is not

OK." Asked what she would advise her daughter in regard to sex, Millie answered, "I would want her to be sure of herself in a relationship, not have casual relationships. I want her to live in a nice world." Here are echoes of her old idealistic quest—her search for the nice world.

Millie's identity status at age thirty-four appears to be Identity Diffusion with some elements of return to a Foreclosure position. She has become the person she is largely by default. Not knowing what else to do or to believe, she has chosen to accept what fell to her and tried to adapt. She is clearly disappointed that she is not working but bravely trying to rationalize a career out of motherhood. She will teach her children the Catholicism she tried to escape from because she was unable to find another belief system that works for her. She has increasingly come to feel that the world may not be a nice place and that she may have no meaningful place in it. Now her hopes are that she can somehow create a nice world for her children.

During this interview, Millie spoke as she had in college of the woman who was dying of cancer and inspired her interest in cancer research. Again, she became tearful telling this story. "That's when I got a goal." But now the goal seems unattainable. When we view Millie's frustrated occupational searches through a psychological lens, it appears that some highly grandiose illusion was triggered during her childhood—an illusion that remained important to her emotionally but could not be satisfied by any reality. Running through Millie's job questing is the sense that she was continually directed by the fantasy of stepping into highly responsible positions where she could make important contributions but without doing the background work of increasing her skills or moving up through the ranks. When these jobs failed to offer her the anticipated glory, she became disillusioned and dissatisfied. In this sense, her goals, although they sounded realistic in college, were fantasy dominated rather than under the control of her reality ego.

At the same time, Millie was seeking from her employment relationships with people that would build her self-esteem. Continually, when she described her job experiences, she focused more on the quality of her relationships with her co-workers than on the work itself. She was happy to do even menial jobs as long as people made her feel good about herself, liked and admired her.

Disappointment similarly marked her relationships with her friends. She wanted friends to be like family members, but friends put their own interests first. She therefore did not trust Philip when she first met him. When he asked her to live with him, she was frightened. "I felt dependent and uncomfortable moving into his territory. What happens if we got on each other's nerves? I have nowhere to go." When they began to feel increasingly committed to each other, she was frightened of making a formal commitment, nervous about the thought of "forever after." But, when she turned twenty-eight, she felt her biological clock running out, was thinking increasingly of children, and they married quickly. "I was crazy about him. I felt we were psychically linked. I feel like we're two halves of a whole."

Philip is a carpenter and had not gone to college. Millie describes him as a "very solid kind of guy." They are both family oriented. "I have more emotional swings; he's more of a stabilizing person." He is, however, more impulsive about spending and more of a dreamer, having what she considers to be wild ideas about business ventures. They argue about spending money, of which they are often short, but enjoy quiet, affectionate evenings at home together.

Millie feels that marriage caused her to become more responsible and more oriented to the future than she was before. At present, she is struggling with feeling dependent on Philip. She feels that it is hard to maintain a sense of herself, especially since becoming a mother. She feels less "equal" because she is not working and finds herself backing off from responsibility and decision making because she is not earning money. "I feel more defensive about me as an entity, a separate person." She feels unequal to Philip because he is the breadwinner, and she feels subordinate to her child, whose needs must come first. She recognizes that it would all be easier if she went back to work but does not want someone else raising her children. In a recent period of stress in the marriage, Philip began to think of relocating and starting over in his job. She found that with one child and another on the way, she wanted the stability of a familiar environment and family close by. The thought of moving threw her into a panic, and she was frightened to think about how helpless she had become. "I feel tossed around being tied to someone else's whims and someone else's schedule."

Consistent with the impulsivity that has governed Millie's life since college, both of her pregnancies were unplanned. When she became pregnant with her first child, she was not sure she was ready for motherhood, but she had already had two abortions and did not want to have a third. She and her husband decided to become parents. "Nobody could have told me the joy I would experience. I am amazed at the breadth and depth of my feelings." She had thought of returning to work after six weeks, but "once I had her, the thought of giving her up to some stranger was just—I couldn't do it."

She enjoys the time she spends with her three-year-old daughter, but each new stage of her child's development makes Millie feel anxious and unprepared. In tones similar to those she used when speaking of her marriage, Millie described the way in which becoming a mother has made her feel more responsible. She is now conscious of herself as a role model, feels she must be careful about her language and her manners. Despite her wistfulness about her vanished career goals, she feels that motherhood has been extemely rewarding. "I was crazy in love with Philip. I'm crazy in love with my daughter. It makes me feel good about myself that I'm capable of feeling such strong emotions. It makes me feel like a good human being that I can feel such things."

Her views of raising children are much the same as those of her parents, especially the idea of wanting to instill a strong sense of right and wrong. "I would like her to excel in something. She's very bright, and I think she could really do something, really make a contribution to whatever she wanted to do." One notes here the transfer of unfulfilled ambitions.

At thirty-four, Millie is still in search of self-esteem, now hoping to find it in motherhood. She has never adequately internalized a sense of self-worth, partly because her dreams have been so far from what she was capable of accomplishing. This conflict over self-esteem is epitomized in the earliest memory she reported in this later interview: "Being in kindergarten. We were cutting out shamrocks. The teacher asked me to cut out the shamrock, and I was so impressed that she asked me to cut it out. This was going to be the best shamrock the world had ever seen. I was being so careful that I was going too slow, and she ended up coming over and taking it out of my hands and saying, 'OK, we'll let someone else do this.' I was crushed." This poignant memory encapsulates the psychological struggle Millie has experienced throughout her life. The theme of the "best the world has ever seen" has pervaded Millie's psychological life since childhood, and she has never quite figured out how to put her actions and aspirations together. She dreams of greatness and is continually disappointed to find herself only real.

Her second earliest memory concerns another important, related theme in Millie's development, the wish to be grown up: "First grade. My mother had bought me a little birthstone ring— a real stone—my first piece of jewelry. I felt, 'Wow! I must be a big girl now.' Somehow it came off and got lost. I was really upset. It was my most prized possession. I was trying to find the ring, and one of my friends questioned whether it was really my ring since it was too big anyway. I felt really bad because I had lost the ring, felt responsible for losing something my mother had entrusted me with. She thought I was old enough, and I lost it. I also felt bad that my friend had said that."

The same anxieties continue to underlie Millie's current worries. Even as a young adult, Millie has had difficulty feeling grown up. She both feared and welcomed marriage because of its association with grown-up status, but could not bring herself to decide to have a child. Now that she is a mother, her anxieties focus on how to handle each stage of development, as though she somehow is still not grown up enough to have such responsibility.

Millie traces the source of her disillusionment with life to her having to learn that there are bad people in the world. She remembers college as a happy time when she was free to do and say what she wanted. She felt "in tune with myself," free to express herself and to be crazy if she wanted to. This epoch ended when, while working as a taxi driver, she learned that there were some people in the world who would cheat, harm, and threaten her. "I stopped seeing myself as 'everybody's like me' " and began seeing herself as a potential victim. She felt unprotected, and this aspect of her childhood, the sense of being protected, of being in a world where someone will always see that things come out all right, was an aspect she was not ready to relinquish.

Too many times, Millie felt that she had had the "wind knocked out of my sails" by disappointments in her jobs, her friends, humanity. The underlying fantasy here seems to be that she was the good, innocent being who always meant well in a world that is evil and threatening. As a result, Millie grew close again to her family and became grateful to them. With them she could count on the love and protection she assumed she would find but failed to find in the larger world. She now feels close to her family, although she sees them only several times a year. Most important, she has moved close to them internally, feeling that the values they gave her, the way they raised her, were right after all. She thinks lovingly of her parents as her heritage, as where she came from, and they are among the most important people in her life. She sees herself as always having been the weirdo of the family because she would cut loose and be fierce about her independence. Her parents are still a little afraid of that in her, that she might cut loose again. And she does still feel the old tugs and pulls between her wishes for adventure and her needs for stability. But for now she is choosing stability.

Millie's disappointment in her close friends has also brought her back to her family. Her friends were not there for her when she needed them emotionally, and she has become reserved about friendship. All the people that Millie now feels closest to are family members. "I have some friends," she says, "but they are not a major influence in my life." She contrasts this situation to her college experience, when friends were like an extended family to her. Again, there is the sense of welcome retreat into a safe world of family; Millie has felt bruised and scarred by the outside world.

Disenchanted with work, hopeless about friendship, Millie

now defines the core of herself around her capacity to feel. "At the times that I feel that my life stinks and I can't take it any more, I think that as long as I can still feel, I'm OK. I'm still a human being, still functioning. I tap into my reserve supply of strength; there are times that you know that you have to be strong." The major source of identity for her right now is her capacity to experience love and joy; this capacity makes her feel like a full human being.

When she thinks of her future, she thinks of having more time for herself and not having to be so entirely devoted to her family. She forgets here that when she did have time to herself, she felt lost and helpless. She worries, however, about how it will be when her children grow up, finding it hard to imagine that she could ever disentangle herself from them.

We observe in Millie a number of themes, some of which are unique to her, some of which are common to women who have undergone a protracted Moratorium period. Most typical of the (college-age) Moratoriums is the focus on feeling. These are women who fully experience their lives and revel in their emotions. Millie exemplifies this theme in the extreme: She defines herself by what she feels. This focus on feeling leaves them open to intense and often unresolvable ambivalence; life becomes a process of swinging from one pole to the other. For Millie, the poles have been her adventurousness and her needs for roots. Unable to comfortably opt for one side or the other, unable to integrate these aspects of herself, Millie avoids decisions and allows things to happen to her. Each of the important decisions in her life—the move to Florida, her move back home, her jobs, her marriage, her pregnancies—has been a spur-of-the-moment decision that she later rationalizes and adapts to. As she says, she does not research things very well.

While they were in college, Moratorium women were seen to share a common underlying set of grandiose fantasies and a feeling that reality is dry and mundane in comparison. Millie clearly illustrates this dynamic theme. Even as a child, she wanted to be the best and most special, was preoccupied with reexperiencing this self-glorified ego state. Her life has been a continual series of disappointments as these dreams do not ma-

terialize, but her experiences in reality do not alter her fundamental needs for glory. Her grandiose fantasies, which moved
from shamrocks as a child to a cure for cancer as an adolescent, are now centered on her daughter, who she (fairly consciously) hopes will become what she failed at being. At this
point, her narcissistic ideals change direction but are not modu-
lated.

While Millie has not been able to use her disappointments
to modify her goals and make them more realizable, she has also
accumulated a good deal of rage as a result of what she experiences as her failure to fulfill her dreams. In each instance, however, the rage is externalized, as she becomes increasingly angry
at the world, which has, in her view, prevented her from doing
the great things she always imagined she would do.

Although Millie continues to struggle with the same developmental problems, she has nevertheless grown and matured.
Individuation has taken place. She calls this change her struggle
against egocentricity, and what she means is that she increasingly experiences herself as separate from other people. Her life
experiences have wrought in her an understanding that others
are not extensions of herself and that she is not an extension of
them, and this appears to have been the hard-won lesson of a
slow process of growth. Part of Millie remains, however, in need
of merger, which she imagines herself to have with her husband
—with whom she feels "psychically linked"—and with her daughter, whom she is unable to leave and whose needs must never go
unmet, regardless of the cost to herself. Therefore, although
Millie is somewhat more differentiated from the rest of the
world than she was, she continues to need an intense, boundary-
shattering connectedness to others.

When Millie does have this intense connectedness, she begins to fear for her independent side. In this sense, she is replay-
ing her adolescent struggles but at an adult level. Unique to
Millie is that the poles of her struggle of independence/merger
are so unmodulated. When she is independent, she must "cut
loose," "be crazy"; when she is close to another, she must feel
"as one" or as "two halves of a whole."

In a major sense, Millie appears to be trying to go home

again. Although it is difficult to say precisely where she ought to be ranked in identity status, she seems to be trying to return to a Foreclosure position. Maybe all those old values were right after all, thinks Millie, as she tries to make a life for herself much like her mother's, taking care of children and home, getting involved in the church, and doing crafts. Her failure at making a clear life-style of her own leaves her at least grateful that she has internalized something else to fall back on, and this is what she, like several other Moratorium women, has done.

Meredith

This phenomenon of going home again is, in fact, clearer in the case of Meredith, who did not make the protracted and painful effort to define herself that Millie did, who reclaimed her heritage much sooner.

Meredith grew up in a rural area of Maine. Her father was a lobsterman, her mother a lobsterman's wife. Neither parent had finished high school, but they were eager for their children to be educated. Meredith planned to be an elementary schoolteacher. Her parents were not religious but sent her to the local Lutheran church out of a sense of propriety. Meredith's Moratorium status in college grew out of her conflicts about sexual values. She saw her upbringing as puritanical and was therefore in much conflict about the common sexual behavior at her small women's college. Sexual behavior became a basis for her to differentiate herself from her background, but she was having sexual relations with her fiance with an enormous amount of guilt. She felt unable to resolve the question of what she believed and unable to please both her family and her fiance. Her decision to have a sexual relationship "once in awhile" with her fiance, however, seemed at the time to be a step in the direction of some autonomy, albeit guilt producing.

In her college interview, Meredith remembered her childhood as a happy one, despite a strict, punitive mother. Her mother's strong opinions were still important to her, but she was trying to form some of her own. As a child, Meredith had been with her mother almost constantly and was finding it hard, as a late adolescent, to move away from her influence. Meredith's father was a hard worker who had no interests outside the family. He resented her having boyfriends, saw boys as a threat to the intactness of his family: They might take her away. He was a demanding man, accustomed to having his own way.

Meredith saw herself as having been a shy and inhibited child who took great joy in her academic successes. She loved to be asked to stay after school to help the teacher wash the blackboards and was proud of the attention she received for being bright.

Going away to college was "eye opening" to her, as she had had no preparation for the diversity of backgrounds and values she would encounter. John, her fiance, whom she met during her first year at college, offered her stability and comfort in the face of these pressures. Her mother had always warned her about men taking advantage of her, and with John she felt secure that this was not happening. Although she was not in love with him and they did not have a romantic relationship, she felt that she was being realistic in choosing him. He was a man she felt she could manipulate to her own wishes and could talk out of his traditional views of women's roles.

At the end of college, then, Meredith was just leaning out over the edge of her basically Foreclosure pattern of identity, experimenting with some differences of thought and behavior, and paying the price in guilt.

Once married, a year later, however, the conflict that might have been a development-inducing one subsided as Meredith and John began to build a traditional life together. By age thirty-two, Meredith had brought herself and her husband home. She has since become a schoolteacher and gotten the master's degree that John had not thought necessary for a woman; she organizes her life around their relationship and her teaching. They would like to have children, but she has had difficulty conceiving. They lead an active life, full of sports activities, full of warmth and companionship, although she sometimes resents John's passivity about doing chores around the house.

The only remnant of Meredith's college-age effort to take a stand different from that of her internalized parents is her dedication to being taken seriously as a woman in her profession. She is sensitive to this issue and will do battle for it. Otherwise, she has remained close, both in her everyday life and in values, to her parents. She says, disingenuously, that she is just like them. Meredith, then, is much like the Foreclosures in her emphasis on responsibility and being good; she is not at all self-reflective. She has few friends, preferring the association and closeness with her husband and her family. The eye-opening experiences of college are now like a half-forgotten dream.

Other Moratoriums

Like Meredith, three other women who had been classified as Moratorium in college and Foreclosure/Achievement in adulthood went home again via an early marriage. For them, marriage was a way of going back to mother, both literally and symbolically. One woman, married now ten years, stressed proudly throughout her interview that her mother is her best friend, has been the most important person in her life, and influences her in all things.

Another woman, whose mother suffered from severe emotional illness, finds maternal gratification in her husband. "I can't imagine anything I would want of marriage that isn't there. Ken is a caring, loving, supportive man. I think in every area of my life he has a part, he has a place. I can't think of any area that is not fulfilled or could be better. We are open and honest with each other. If we have something to talk about, something we are worried about or are afraid of, we can go to each other and talk about it. It's never yelling or criticism; it's never the harshness that can be there in some marriages. We respect each other, and that's a big part of why we're able to have such a good marriage. I think of Ken as my best friend, and I think this is a formula that could be well used by others. I think we fulfill each other's needs because we want to, not because we have to, not because of some piece of paper saying we have to be something for another person. If I wished it to be different in any way it would be the time constraints that are put on our marriage by our jobs. We both go into withdrawal after vacations, after spending so much time together. I feel unhappy not being with him all the time, and he does too." This woman and her husband have decided not to have children because they could not bear the separation between them that that would entail. "We're our own children; we indulge ourselves and each other, and if we had another person there, we wouldn't be able to be there always for each other."

"Be there always for each other" is the fantasy of ultimate and continuing union that so clearly pervades the mental life of the Foreclosures. But these particular women, unlike the Foreclosures, were loosening childhood ties somewhat during their adolescence. Unlike the Foreclosures, they had been more successful as teenagers, more sociable, more popular, more interpersonally confident. It appears, from these data, that Moratorium women frighten themselves by their efforts to separate. Their ambivalence during the separation struggle is intense, and they defend against it by trying to cling to someone. They all speak of having looked at options during college, of being shocked and excited by possibilities, but these six women were unable to make use of them. In the end, they opted for safety. However, none of these women, with the exception of Millie, express regrets about that decision. They are happy with their lives, optimistic about the future, much like the Foreclosures.

Moratorium to Achievement

While six of the ten Moratoriums have formed identities based on childhood values, following the path of either Millie or Meredith, three have become clearly defined Identity Achievements, and one remains in the Moratorium status at age thirty-four. The life course of one of the Moratorium-to-Achievement women, Marlene, demonstrates how rocky and frightening the road can be.

Marlene

Marlene in College. Marlene grew up in a small town outside Philadelphia and chose to attend a small women's college because of the influence of some friends a few years older than she. Although majoring in sociology, she intended to get some experience and see what different fields were like before she chose work goals for herself. She chose her major because she liked the people who were in that department.

Marlene was raised Jewish but without any strong sense of religious feeling. She did have a vivid sense of roots, however, and Jewish culture and heritage were important to her. Her major beliefs were in some vaguely defined sense of humanism, but she said she never had any strong convictions one way or the other.

Politically, she had flirted with Leftist politics until she came to dislike the people in the movement. From here, she got somewhat involved in the women's movement but was not yet clear on how she felt about these issues. She seemed to see herself as propelled into beliefs by circumstances.

Marlene was somewhat more clear on her sexual than on her political values; she had decided to have a sexual relationship with her boyfriend of four years, although she was aware that her parents did not approve of this behavior. She was unable to define this current decision as a standard, however. Because she had never had the opportunity to make such a decision in regard to anyone else, she was uncertain how she would react. Her behavior, in other words, was responsive to a particular relationship, but she had not formed general standards and values in regard to her sexuality.

Clinically, Marlene gave the impression of being an other-directed person, someone sensitive to the attributes, needs, and views of others, someone who accommodated herself to their preferences. Throughout the interview, she emphasized her relationships with others as the source of her own beliefs and feelings. This pattern was not true, however, with respect to her parents. Marlene's parents were Holocaust victims, much older than the parents of her friends, and she had the strong sense that because their background was so different, their attitudes and values had little to do with her. They wanted her to go to college, marry, and have a family, and this much of them she internalized. For the rest, she felt that she had to look outside her home for models and for options for how to conduct the rest of her life.

Throughout college her relationship to others had been most important, particularly the opportunity to debate and to consider different modes of being and thinking. Some of her friends, the ones in the women's movement, for example, got her thinking about what it means to be a woman, questions that had never seriously arisen in her experience before. She found herself having to justify, for example, why she ironed her boyfriend's shirts, and she became quite unsettled when she could not produce a rationale for this behavior that they would accept.

Her boyfriend, Larry, was the most important person to Marlene. She met him during her freshman year at college and saw him as someone who was helping her to experience things. She saw him as intelligent, sensitive, and patient, and he was urging her to be more independent of him, much like a good parent.

An only child, Marlene had a strong sense that her life began once she came to college. She experienced her precollege years as innocent and unaware. She described having gone through a brief period of hating her parents for being so different, for not having taught her to communicate with others, for having given her hang-ups. Even during college, she still found it hard to communicate with them, feeling that they could not understand who she was or how she had grown.

Although she had excelled academically and been a leader in high school, Marlene always felt clearly apart from others. In addition to the religious differences, she never even felt fully American because her parents were immigrants. At the same time, her parents' background made it impossible to want to live the kind of life they had led. During college, then, Marlene was clearly casting about for possibilities and alternatives, alert to others, interested in the choices they were making, but clinging to her boyfriend as a surrogate parent and structuring her life around his.

Looking at material that illuminates unconscious aspects of personality, we see that Marlene had strong fantasies about men being rescuers. Her earliest memory, from age four, was of "playing with this kid who was three, and he would be Mickey Mouse and I would be Minnie Mouse; and, from TV, Minnie would always get kidnapped and tied to a tree, and Mickey would come and rescue her."

Intense oedipal themes were also strongly present unconsciously. The following dream is an example: "It was a sexual dream about a professor. We were in a room having a class, and we took our clothes off. It was no big thing. Just no one had clothes on. And there was something about I was having an affair with this professor, and other professors had found out about it; and people were saying what a horrible thing it was and how they disapproved of the whole thing and I remember specifically the feeling I had knowing I loved this person so intensely but he was married and he wasn't going to leave his wife, and it was just fruitless—just that sense of desperation and frustration and it was really an intense feeling."

Although she saw her father infrequently because of his work schedule, Marlene viewed him as spoiling her and rescuing her from her mother's discipline. Clearly, the fantasy of the strong man as savior was, at this point, an important part of her psychodynamics. Consciously, despite her involvement in the women's movement, Marlene, at the close of her adolescence, saw her life as one that would be directed by a man.

Marlene at Thirty-Three. On reflection, Marlene was aware that she did not choose a vocation in college, partly because she had no strong calling to any particular field. She was mostly invested in Larry and getting him to marry her. She followed him to New York, doing unskilled jobs while he pursued his education. As time went on, he grew increasingly distant, and she finally realized that he was not intending to marry her. Feeling somewhat desperate, she made the impulsive decision to join a college friend who planned to enter a program in paralegal studies. This plan involved a move to Boston, where she spent a rather uneventful year working on the degree only to find no jobs available. With another friend, she moved to California, where she did some odd jobs to tide her over while she thought about what to do next. At the same time, one of her friends got her interested again in women's issues, and she began serving as a volunteer in a women's health center. This job led to her training as a paramedic, and, after six months, she took a part-time job coordinating the clinic, doing crisis intervention and some paramedical work.

Marlene, throughout this time, had continued her interest in Jewish culture and, at a synagogue function, met Ben, a man who was part of a group planning to emigrate to Israel. She was attracted to his apparent sense of purpose, and they began living together. She became involved in his group's project to set up a school for handicapped children in Israel, and she spent the next period of her life committed to this goal. She found, however, to her great disappointment, that the carefully laid plans did not materialize on their arrival in Israel. After a stressful and frustrating year of waiting and trying to negotiate with the administrative authorities, they decided to return to the United States.

Marlene had had stronger hopes pinned on the Israel venture than on any previous undertaking. Partly, Marlene had felt that things "weren't happening here the way I had wanted them to" and partly going to Israel represented a way of reconnecting with her extended family, most of whom were there. She felt Israel was a place where she could settle down. Before going to Israel, she and Ben married, and their child was born there. Their time in Israel was extremely stressful. They were discouraged over the failure of their plans, the difficulty of finding other work, and Marlene was distressed by the difficulty of having a baby according to her own requirements in a foreign culture. These strains were beginning to affect their marriage.

Back in the States, they were unsure what to do. They began staying with relatives and visiting friends. While visiting an old friend who was now living in a small town in Colorado, they impulsively decided to stay there. They liked the area and thought, "Why don't we try this?" They each got part-time jobs and equally divided the childcare. Marlene was able to find work in a law office, until she was laid off a year later. She then found work for a few hours a week in another women's health center. Ben, meanwhile, was having a difficult time deciding on his own career path, and Marlene was becoming increasingly resentful of his checkered employment record and frequent unemployment. She persuaded him to return for further education and began increasing the time she was spending at the health center, which brought increased responsibility and involvement in the activities there.

As Marlene was settling into a committed work life, the marital problems were getting worse. Marlene discovered that Ben was involved in an affair with a woman he met at school. She saw less and less of him and began to feel that they were sharing nothing but the childcare. "I was feeling like it had all fallen apart. I wanted to hang on to what I saw as my family, but it wasn't working out the way I wanted it to."

A women's support group that she had been involved with for a year helped her to sort out some of her feelings and to begin to accept the idea of separation from Ben. It became clear, after some time, that neither one of them was still committed to the relationship, although it was painful for Marlene to give up her hopes for this family. "I had to begin to think in terms of 'What do I do now?', to get it together as a single person." For the first time, Marlene began to think seriously of a career. She found that the medical work she had been doing at the clinic gave her the most satisfaction, and she began considering a career as a midwife. She was systematic about checking out programs and possibilities and found that the program most tailored to her needs was 2,000 miles away. After much agonizing about her decision, she enrolled in this program, leaving her son in the care of his father. Marlene experienced this decision as an epiphany. "For the first time, I felt like I knew what I wanted to do. I remember in college feeling so envious of people who were directed and knew what they wanted to do. Then I suddenly felt that sense of direction at the age of thirty-two, and it felt wonderful. Everything started to fall into place."

When I interviewed Marlene, she was happily engaged in a demanding and prestigious program, working hard, enjoying it, but guilty and worried about her relationship with her son. She felt, however, that there was no way she could take care of her son and fulfill her responsibilities at school. She sees him on vacations. Shortly after moving to New York for her schooling,

Marlene met a man with whom she is now living. She is hopeful about this relationship. Except for missing her son, she is, at present, feeling optimistic and whole.

Looking back, Marlene reflected that she had been clear in college only about wanting a family. She thinks that she perhaps was keeping herself fluid in order to be open to marriage and family. Indeed, all her decisions thereafter, except the final one, were based on the man she felt committed to. She sees now that her need was to "hang on to security above all else." She regrets now that she had not taken seriously the idea of a career for herself earlier. She might have become a doctor. "I was floating here and there and bouncing off of what I was getting from other people. My attitude was 'why not' rather than the sense of what to do." The important discovery for her was that she could have both a family and a job. Her fantasies about a family made it hard to think about work until she found that she did not have to choose one or the other. (She is hoping to have her son back with her once she completes her training.)

At present, Marlene also has high hopes for her current relationship. She feels that she has learned much from her mistakes. Her first fiance she now sees as having been domineering and herself as needing someone at the time who would take charge of her. With Ben, she did too much taking care of him and came to realize that much of their marriage had been based on mutual assumptions, or misassumptions, that they had not communicated to each other. This time, she again feels in love but experiences much greater communication and openness in the relationship than she ever has before. She is again thinking about a family, but this time "getting it all in."

Since she left college, both of Marlene's parents have died, and the loss of them is probably part of what underlies her strong need to create a new family. Despite her growing interests in her career, relationships are still central to her life.

Marlene believes that her group of feminist women friends were a major force behind the changes she has made in the past two years. She sees this time as having been a period of "emerging" and feels that she could not have done it without the support of her friends. "If I can perceive how someone else perceives me, it helps me to pull things together." Despite their physical distance, they have been strongly internalized and she feels their continued presence. In psychological terms, she seems to have found replacement internal others to please, and on them can she base her self-esteem.

From this vantage point in her development, Marlene reflects that she always had wanted a stable life and the kind of family she never had as a child, a family close to a "TV kind of image." She recognizes that many of her decisions were made to fulfill that hope but realizes also that perhaps she did not fully want that life because she has done many things that have taken her along a different path. An insightful and self-reflective woman, Marlene sees now that she has done many things for the wrong or for unexamined reasons but now feels more fully in touch with herself and more optimistic than she has ever felt before.

Moratoriums as a Group

Marlene exemplifies a Moratorium odyssey that seems, at this point, at least, to have been successful. Her life course thus far has led her in the direction of increased self-knowledge and clarity about herself and her goals. Marlene, like Millie, had cut loose from the ties of childhood during college. Both found boyfriends as substitutes for their parents and thought that they were headed in different directions from those of their childhoods. Both Marlene and Millie experienced intense disappointments in their hopes for life after college, yet Marlene has struggled forward toward an Achieved identity, while Millie has retreated.

An examination of the differences between them can perhaps shed some light on those factors that determine the outcome of a Moratorium phase for women. Whereas Millie gave up in the face of frustration, Marlene kept trying. For Millie, the causes of her disappointments were all externalized. She came to blame the world for her failures, which left her feeling free of self-blame but helpless in the face of an uncontrollable world. Marlene, by contrast, learned to internalize her failures without destroying her self-esteem. She was able to accept responsibility for what went wrong and to learn to live with guilt.

The capacity to tolerate and integrate guilt appears to be central to those who successfully parlay Moratorium states into Identity Achievement. To be different from one's family or even to be like one's family on one's own terms involves a measure of guilt as the self disengages from old but persistent notions of a "good" girl.

When we view the Moratoriums as a group during college, guilt is the omnipresent theme among them. They are struggling at this point to try to untangle their familial ties, doing things they know their families would not approve of, and finding various means to deal with the resulting guilt. One frequently chosen way is to find a boyfriend who will offer support or a new value system. Frequently these boyfriends are even more controlling than the woman's parents, but because they are not parents, their control is more palatable or even welcomed. By pleasing these boyfriends, Moratoriums can partly assuage the guilt about not pleasing their parents.

Moratorium women, during college, describe themselves as having had overprotective mothers who indulged and overvalued them. As one woman put it, "I'm all she has, and now she has nothing left." At the height of the separation struggle, they seem to feel like infidels who have betrayed their mothers' love. Many had mothers whom they consciously wanted not to be like, and their effort to disavow their dependence on their mothers was an effort to ensure becoming unlike them. And becoming unlike mother was, in turn, a way of denying dependence.

At the same time as this group rejected their identifications with their mothers, they tended to idealize their fathers, betraying their mothers a second time. Seen as strong and authoritarian although warm and loving, their fathers represented a romanticized ideal of strength and success. More than any of the other groups during college, the Moratoriums reported daydreams, often continuing from childhood, of wondrous successes. To be an opera star, to be an ambassador to Russia, to discover a cure for cancer—these were the fantasies that filled the heads of the little girls they once were. (The Achievements' daydreams, by contrast, were much less specific and unique.) Frequently, fathers seemed to be the source of the glorified aspirations Moratorium women had for themselves, although more for the tone of their goals than for the content. To be "right" was important. Because these aspirations were felt by the Moratoriums as a necessity for some sort of idealized perfection, they could only again suffer guilt, this time at having disappointed their own hopes.

This, then, was the Moratorium dilemma at the end of college. They suffered guilt for violating the (largely sexual) prohibitions of their mother and guilt for not attaining the ideals of their father, and they could find no neutral stronghold to rest on.

For these women, at the end of college, goals tended to be formulated in an imperious, totalistic way. They sought "the answers." From childhood, they had derived satisfaction and self-esteem from being "right," and through adolescence they remained convinced of the essential rightness of themselves, their families, and their beliefs. The shock at finding other modes of rightness that cannot, of course, all be right seems to induce the Moratorium state. As for Millie, this realization prompts or promotes the autonomy struggle from the parents. Instead of liberalizing the demanding ideals (as an Achievement eventually does), a Moratorium embarks on a kind of crusade, determined to discover what is "really right," and, until she can find something to embrace or gives up the quest, she can make no choices around which to construct an identity.

To separate and individuate from parents and their trusted standard of rightness means bearing guilt. Those who, like Marlene, were able to find a way to bear the guilt, went on to achieve identities. Those who, like Meredith and Millie, were unable to tolerate the guilt, made choices that would quell it. Strikingly, although, while in college, Moratorium women were the group most critical of their mothers, they were, twelve years later, the closest to their mothers of any of the identity-status groups. Evidently, the tie to mother had been, for these women, so intense that it was a difficult one from which to disengage. They tried to do it by moving far away (internally at least), not being close to her any more. But this road, in the end, led back to her. What they could not succeed in fighting, the Moratoriums joined.

Another striking commonality among the college-age Moratoriums was their single-minded focus on and need for relationships. Unlike the Achievements, who looked to both their own capacities and to significant relationships to bolster self-esteem, the Moratoriums showed little purposeful investment in personal achievement. They experienced themselves, during college, primarily in relation to other people—gaining approval or respect or love, being used, being left, being taught. Here is how they typically described their experiences during college: "I sort of bend towards people. But I have such varied friends that there's always opposition pounding at me." "I met some new people who molded me in a different way. It was confusing because I wasn't sure how I fit in with them, and I found myself becoming like them." "I wanted to be like the girl across the hall, who was secure and didn't need to have people telling her all the time that they like her." "I'm attracted to confident people who make me feel sure they're doing the right thing."

Whereas the Foreclosures were mainly in search of others to replace a lost sense of security, Moratoriums, during college, were most in need of others for new identifications. In talking of their relationships to boyfriends, for example, Moratoriums were not interested in having security but in having their boyfriends show them how to be and to approve of them. Similarly, their interest in women friends was mainly a quest for models, for ideas on how to live. Marlene followed both Larry and Ben in hopes not so much of being taken care of but of having a structure around which to build her own life. Meredith had hoped that her husband would forge new alternatives for her but chose someone as traditional as she and her family had been. Having had no one's lead to follow toward a different way of being, she took the familiar road.

The Identity Achievements also underwent a Moratorium period at some point before they left college; such a period is, in fact, part of the definition of that status. Therefore, it seems, college-age Moratoriums and Achievements ought to be quite alike, as indeed they are among men. Why, then, are there so many differences between Achievement and Moratorium college women? Why should it make a difference if one is still in a Moratorium state during the senior year of college or has passed through one previously?

One possibility is that as the end of college approaches, the social pressures to resolve matters, to make a plan for the future, have a profound influence on those who are going to do so and can do so fairly easily. Not having a life plan is unsettling to women and brings with it anxiety and guilt. Those who affect resolutions of conflict by the end of college appear to be those who have the internal resources to respond to the external necessity of deciding. Those who remain Moratoriums at the end of college appear to be caught in conflict, unable to transcend it. The identity crisis itself, then, appears to be experienced differently within these different personality structures. Those who remained Moratoriums at the end of college included those who were attempting more than the Achievements and those who were attempting less. The Moratoriums who were attempting more were questioning all aspects of their lives, keeping themselves open to possibilities, taking nothing for granted. Those who went on to forge Achieved identities, like Marlene, took several years to do so. They needed additional time and experiences to make up their minds.

Those Moratorium women who were attempting less, like Meredith, experienced crisis only in a circumscribed area of their lives. Possibly they somehow knew all along that they would live out the values and lives derived from their families but were using the college years as a brief vacation from their true selves. Knowing in some deep way the roads their lives would follow, they could use their college independence to be a little different, to try on a new way of being without having such experiences fundamentally modify the people they knew themselves to be. As a result, these women tended to experience a great amount of anxiety and guilt during college, as is typical of the Moratoriums, but the anxiety was a fear of being found out. Such women worried terribly that their parents would discover their sexual behavior or pot smoking, and, in hiding these behaviors from their parents, these women hid their behavior from themselves.

The underlying dimension among the Moratoriums, then, appears to be how much one will allow one's new experiences to be profoundly meaningful. Many times in life a person does things that are out of character. Some people respond to such events by dismissing their importance, saying, "Well, I was on vacation" or "I was drunk" or "I didn't mean what I said." Other people, having the same experiences, reflect deeply about them and alter their self-image to include a self that can behave in such a way. The essence of the Moratorium phase is how much one "means it," and often a woman does not know until a good deal later whether she did or did not.

The process of growth is one of making minute changes that may feel like big risks at the time. We tend to change in small increments, making sure that we have not burned our bridges behind us. Often, we unconsciously arrange for someone to function as a kind of savings bank. We deposit our old self in them for safekeeping, trusting them to hold it for us if we decide to come back to claim it. Many of the Moratorium women spoke of this process. In describing the ways in which they thought their parents expected them to be, they were describing old selves, ways they used to be. They could then have the luxury of experiencing their growth as an external battle, between themselves and their parents, rather than inside themselves. In addition, they knew that their parents were holding the old selves for them, just in case they ever decided to return, which is exactly what many of them did.

For the Moratoriums, the presence of supportive others appears to be necessary in consolidating an independent identity. During college, there is an almost desperate quality to the Moratorium's search for others against whom to define and differentiate herself, and for others to enlist in support of her emerging identity. Each relationship provides raw material for the endless introspection that often marks the Moratoriums, and they tend to ruminate a great deal over how they "really" felt or how they are the same as or different from those they know—all in an effort to discover themselves. After college, however, this built-in support group disperses, and the not-yet-formulated identity is left to flounder. If the identity-formation process (at least, in its first resolution) is not yet completed by graduation, a woman may then experience extreme pressure to return to the safety of the gratifications she experienced in childhood. This process was seen in Meredith, whose budding Moratorium period did not outlast the college environment. Millie searched fruitlessly for some years for friends who would continue to help her define herself, to complete her Moratorium phase, but ended up returning home psychologically, in despair.

Marlene was ultimately able to take charge of her life when friends in the women's support group encouraged her nascent wishes to structure her life on her own terms. The two other women who came through the Moratorium phase with achieved identities similarly found supportive others who helped them to deal with the guilt and uncertainty, not by taking care of them, but through emotional support and validation.

Moratorium women are much more insightful, self-reflective, and internally sensitive people than those in any of the other groups. In some ways, they are the most moving because of their intense emotional experience and capacity for self-analysis. They are the women one most often reads about in popular magazines because they struggle with issues and can talk about their lives and feelings. They are also women who are perpetually in conflict. Apparently, once the Moratorium period has been undertaken, ambivalence can be laid to rest only with great difficulty. Some Moratorium women, such as Meredith, have overcome ambivalence by realizing their dreams in marriage and family harmony. Most of them, however, are still alive to internal conflict, even when they have made choices. Millie, Marlene, and others like them have chosen, more or less willingly, the selves that they have become but continue to suffer, however discreetly, for the selves they did not become.

Chapter 7

Lost and Sometimes Found: The Identity Diffusions

"What shall I do now? What shall I do?"
"I shall rush out as I am, and walk the street
"With my hair down, so. What shall we do to-mor-
    row?
"What shall we ever do?"
                    —*T. S. Eliot,* "The Waste Land"

While in college, women in states of Identity Diffusion consti-
tuted a varied and complex group. Recall that Identity Diffusion is defined by the absence of attributes—no crisis, no commitment. Because more factors can lead to the nonoccurrence
of a developmental accomplishment than to its occurrence, it is
not surprising that Identity Diffusions are the most mixed and
the hardest to understand as a whole group. These women were
adrift and lost, but lost for different reasons.

Women in the Identity Diffusion group are consistently
lowest, among the four identity status groups, on all measures
of healthy psychological functioning. Their overall ego development is low (Hopkins, 1982), and they have more difficulty
forming intimate relationships (Kacerguis and Adams, 1980).
They are highest in anxiety (Schenkel and Marcia, 1972), most

undifferentiated in sex-role orientation (Orlofsky, 1977), and most field dependent (Schenkel, 1975). A critical review of approximately thirty studies using the identity-status paradigm concluded that the most we know about Diffusions is that they tend to withdraw from situations (Bourne, 1978b). We know, then, that Identity Diffusions are bringing up the rear of the developmental continuum in late adolescence. But we know little about why they are having so much difficulty or what becomes of them as adults.

Erikson considered Identity Diffusion to be an unstable state, for where the person fails to claim an identity, society tends to provide one. Often, this failure of choice leads to the individual's being labeled "deviant," and this deviance may become her passively accepted negative identity. Although recognizing its dangers, Erikson tended to view Identity Diffusion as a passing crisis. It might be unduly prolonged or pathologically aggravated, but Identity Diffusion could still be seen as an episode within a normative developmental stage.

The Identity Diffusion women in this sample, when interviewed as college seniors, were a diverse group. All were Diffuse in identity, but they seemed to be Diffuse in different ways. Four different patterns, or subgroups, of Identity Diffusion emerged: severe psychopathology, previous developmental deficits, Moratorium Diffusion, and Foreclosed Diffusion.

The first two of these subgroups, severe psychopathology and previous developmental deficits, were composed of eight women (of sixteen in this identity status) whose personality structure would fall outside the range of the normative. If viewed by clinical psychology or psychiatry, they would be diagnosed as having borderline personality disorders. For those who fell in these subgroups, issues of identity formation were secondary to more basic, earlier, and more primitive psychological issues. These women carried scars of early severe psychological trauma that continued to plague them into late adolescence. The loss of a favored parent, for example, or early emotional neglect led to a general sense of futility and instability that precluded serious investment in the task of identity formation. By and large, these women had parents with whom they were unable to form lasting, positive identifications. The absence of identity crisis in this group seemed to be attributable to their lack of any solid, workable psychic structure to reorganize. Instead, their entire lives had been characterized by a search for some remedy to the ego deficits caused by such early and far-reaching psychological disturbance. They tried one thing after another, but nothing seemed to work well for them. Impulsive, avoiding guilt at all costs, they were unable to make identity commitments because of the instability and unreliability of their capacity to organize and integrate their experiences. Rather than try to make something of themselves, these women, when they thought of the future at all, wished to try to make something *else* of themselves. As one woman, in a moment of hope, put it, "It isn't necessary to build on the past. You can go outside the past and make a new past." These women, as college seniors, experienced their lives as a succession of events unrelated to each other. They felt themselves to be one person one day, another two weeks hence. To this extent, they were attempting to live outside their own histories, disavowing a past that they could not come to terms with. Identity integration then becomes impossible.

The third subgroup, Moratorium Diffusion, was designed to describe three women who were experiencing some crisis in identity but in areas other than those usually used to define a psychosocial identity. These women were in extreme and active conflict about choices for their lives, but their questions were broader, deeper, and more upsetting than those posed by the Moratoriums. Philosophical questions about the meaning of life plagued them more. They were more experimental than the Moratoriums about trying unusual modes of experiencing, liberally employing drugs, sex, and fringe religious groups to these ends. Often they seemed to move in and out of Moratorium (active searching) and Diffusion (giving up, drifting along) states. Although not passively resigning themselves to impulsivity or amorphousness as were the other Diffusions, their crises were less goal directed, less focused on how to become than were the crises of the Moratorium group.

The fourth subgroup, the Foreclosed Diffusions, was made up of five uncommitted women who were drifting along neither in crisis nor able to make commitments. Acting for the moment, unable to define a consistent direction, they seemed to suffer from atrophy of the will. These women had parents whose identities seemed to have been equally diffuse, and, viewing them as college seniors, the researchers had the impression that they would have been Foreclosures if only their parents had provided them with something to foreclose on. These were women whose parents always left decisions up to them, never pushed them into or out of anything. Yet these daughters seem to have sensed that their parents, rather than encouraging them to be independent, were merely expressing their own lack of convictions and inability to make decisions. Such vacillation seems to have induced their daughters to cling even tighter to them for some small measure of security. The women in the Foreclosed Diffusion group shared a kind of fatalistic passivity, feeling that they had so little control over their lives that there was no point in trying to plan. Rather, they would wait to see what life might have in mind for them, ready to adopt whatever was willing to adopt them.

In a sense, the Identity Diffusion group is one of the most interesting to view from a longitudinal perspective. With the other identity statuses, we could make some reasonably good guesses about the future. With the Identity Diffusions, however, their unpredictability befuddles our capacity to forecast. Headed nowhere at the end of college, where do they go and how do they get there? This group is also of special interest to clinicians because half of them were showing psychological disturbance that interfered with their ability to consider identity-formation issues.

Unsurprisingly, this group shows the most varied outcomes. Among the nine women who could be located for the follow-up study, four outcome patterns emerge: Three women remain Diffuse in identity and appear to have remained Diffuse since college with brief efforts to try to define an identity for themselves, efforts that consistently fail. One woman who is still diffuse is in a period of trying to make commitments and settle down. Three women have made identity commitments but, as we shall see, have made them in a way quite different from those in the other identity-status groups. The fourth out-come is a tragic one. Two of these women died in their late twenties. One woman, one of the brightest and most thought-ful women in the original sample, was unable to take hold of any life plan. After college, she lapsed into a deepening de-pression that led to her suicide. On the other deceased woman, no information is available.

Women who were classified as Diffusions have, without question, become the most unusual people in the sample. Their lives most frequently have the quality of gothic novels; they make more unlikely choices and try to live with them. Statisti-cally, Diffusions, as a group, have held more jobs and moved their residences significantly more than those in any of the other groups. In general, they have experienced more and made more changes.

Still-Diffuse Diffusions

Three women could best be classified as still-diffuse Dif-fusions. All had been categorized in the subgroups of severe psy-chopathology or previous developmental deficits at the time of the analysis ten years earlier. The following case exemplifies a life history typical of this subgroup.

Susan

Susan in College. When interviewed at the end of college, Susan showed the fragmented, disorganized approach to life characteristic of the "pure" Diffusions—that is, she was diffuse in each identity category. An art major, she had no plans for after graduation and felt that it was unimportant what she did as long as she did something. She did not hope to marry. "I have more fun not married," she said, "and you can spend all the money on yourself, and you don't get saddled down with responsibilities."

Susan had no religious beliefs at that time. Her father had forced her to go to his church, while her mother had pushed her to another. Her mother's counsel, though, was to wait until she married to choose a religion. For a while, Susan had been in- volved in Eastern mysticism, but "it got too weird. I kind of got into it—not that I believed in it or anything."

On politics, Susan had no ideas at all. "I don't like to vote, and, anyway, I don't know where to vote." Her parents never discussed politics, and there were no issues on which she had strong opinions.

Susan's sexual standards were equally diffuse. Her deci- sions about whether to have sexual intercourse or not were based on whether she liked the man and whether he was good- looking. As she tried to define her standards, she became in- creasingly confused and ended up saying, "I don't know—I hide a lot—think about something else."

This identity-status interview clearly portrayed a scat- tered young woman, unable to define herself on any issue and relatively untroubled about it.

Susan's parents, neither of whom were college graduates, divorced when Susan was in her late teens. She described her mother as "really nice—she'd help me out if I needed it." Al- though closer to her mother than to her father, Susan did not feel she could confide in her or talk to her about serious things and, as a result, saw her only rarely. The youngest of three girls, Susan saw the family dynamics as mother catering to the middle child, father to the oldest, and she being left out. She saw her mother as conservative in her values, especially with regard to sex. "I used to believe like that. A year ago, if somebody would have told me I'd be living with a guy, I wouldn't have believed it. This last year I got messed up somewhere along the line."

With her father, Susan had had for some years "only a fi- nancial relationship." He was at work most of the time when she was growing up, and Susan had little sense of knowing him. She was clear, however, that she wanted to be different from him in every way possible.

Susan admired her two sisters, especially their looks and clothes. Growing up, her heroes were fashion models and movie stars and Scarlett O'Hara because "she always thought about herself, always came first."

At the time of the interview, Susan's emotional energies

were centered on a highly ambivalent relationship with her live-in boyfriend, whom she referred to as Dummy throughout the discussion. He mistreated her in many ways, including turning their apartment into a kind of a commune for his friends where the main activities were drugs and sex. She was fitfully trying to summon the resources to leave him. Susan's previous experiences with men had been largely fantasy dominated, with many crushes on unavailable men. Her few previous real involvements ended abruptly when the man "split."

In general, Susan presented a portrait of great emotional impoverishment. Her earliest memory was: "Probably singing to the cows. That must have been age six or seven. I always showed the cows everything I got new, plus I'd sing to them." In this memory is expressed both her difficulties in human relationships as well as the narcissism revealed directly in her movie-star fantasies.

Although, clinically, Susan appeared to be suffering from serious psychological disorder, she was nevertheless functioning. Her impulsive, self-indulgent, and self-protective approach to life was under enough control to make it possible for her to continue in college without psychotherapeutic intervention.

Susan at Thirty-Four. Upon her graduation from college, Susan's aunt found her her first job—teaching art in an alternative school for which an education degree was not necessary. Susan enjoyed this job, but it was short-lived because the school closed for lack of funds. She then moved to Arizona, where she had a friend, and unsuccessfully looked for another teaching job. Since then, she has knocked about, trying a variety of relatively unskilled jobs; for the past five years, she has been working as a cashier, back in her hometown.

Susan continued her pattern of unpredictable relationships with men who mistreated her in one way or another until two years ago when she found a special man whom she felt would change her life and whom she wanted to marry. She began converting to Catholicism in preparation for their marriage, but he left her abruptly after she announced to him that she was pregnant. Susan had decided to have the baby even though she was in no financial position to care for one. Tragically, the baby was born with severe congenital defects and lived only three months. This difficult time of stress led to a religious mystical experience, including visions, and Susan became a devout Catholic.

The church has become, at least for now, a center of Susan's life. She answered many of the current questions by referring to her religious beliefs, as though she had truly experienced her conversion as a rebirth. Christ, she says, as well as her priest, are the most important people in her life.

At present, Susan is living with her mother because the unsteadiness of her work does not provide her with enough money to live on her own. Her mother is also helping her to manage money, something Susan has never done very well. Susan still wishes for a career, instead of these "measly jobs," but seems to have no idea how to go about getting one.

Despite this rather depressing picture, Susan does not seem depressed (at least superficially). She has a number of friends with whom she enjoys good times, and the major good experiences in her life center around pleasurable interactions with friends. Of her life goals now, Susan summarizes, reflectively, "Here I am—I'm still thinking—I'll get a job, then I'll get married. That's terrible . . . I'm *still* thinking . . . that really is." Susan's romantic fantasies have not come true. The overall feeling about her is of a very childlike person, wandering among the fragments of her life.

Other Still-Diffuse Diffusions

Like the other two still-diffuse Diffusions, Susan has difficulty being reflective or evaluating her life. Meaning exists at the moment. One of the other still-diffuse women is currently engaged in an effort to research careers and figure out what she wants to do. This plan sounded promising, largely because of her enthusiasm, but further probing unearthed that she has embarked on such projects before, only to have them end in failure. The style of these women is impulsive. Great energy may be invested in an undertaking, but the plan always sours, in part because they do not look too closely at possibilities and they greet each opportunity as salvation. But they remain hopeful that the next person or project that comes along will fulfill their dreams.

The three still-diffuse Diffusions share a lack of personality structure, making them dependent on others to test reality and to think for them. They have found friends or family members to organize around internally and who also help to organize them externally. The deficits that underlay their Identity Diffusion in college are not remedied. It is, in fact, hard to perceive growth or development in these women. Their external circumstances change; they are buffeted or supported by the Fates; but they, internally, remain essentially unchanged.

It is striking that these women all welcomed the interview as an external structuring agent to force them to think about issues they do not usually think about. Interestingly, two of them (including Susan) had brief (two-to-three-month) passes at psychotherapy, which they found "helpful." To them, therapy was one more process that was "tried."

Hardest to find in these women is the source of ego strength that keeps them going. Overall, they seem not to take life too seriously and to be able to lose themselves in a "good time." As one of the other women put it, "I'm doing the things I want to do," mainly sports, recreation, being with friends; she is not troubled about working in a job far below her potential.

All these three women have had unusual experiences that they elevate to the status of personal myth (such as Susan's elaborate telling of the loss of her child). They are colorful, if tragically so, and would, no doubt, be viewed by others as likeable eccentrics. Although they take risks, they are the risks of impulse rather than growth, and life becomes a process of living with the consequences of hastily formed decisions. But, whatever the degree of underlying psychopathology, depression does not overwhelm them. They have their ups and downs, but they bounce back.

The three still-diffuse Diffusions share a history of difficulties in relationships with men. With apparently deeply rooted fears of men, they all choose unusual partners and have a checkered and disappointing series of experiences. Another one of these women has found consistency and stability in a long-distance relationship, one way of dealing with her fears of intimacy. Unable to define a sense of self, these women remain unable to commit themselves to another unless there are certain safeguards of distance or difficulty that prevent the much-feared closeness and commitment. None of them wish to marry or have children but do not rule out its "happening."

In their views of their lives, only the present is real for these women. Unlike women in the other identity statuses, the still-diffuse Diffusions could give only hazy outlines of their lives up to the present issues and struggles. The future is unimaginable, and the past is largely lost. They are not self-analytic women, and the questions they ask of life are basically concrete: How can I get a higher paying or more secure job? Shall I live alone or share an apartment?

Still Diffuse/Trying to Settle Down

These women stand in contrast to another form of continuing Identity Diffuseness, subclassified as Moratorium/Diffusion. This form of Identity Diffusion is quite different from that already described, being much more probing, philosophical, and aware.

Debbie

Debbie in College. Of all the women in the college sample, Debbie was the most articulate. On occupation: "I don't know what I want to do—join the circus, a gypsy camp, I don't know. Yesterday I was thinking of starting a daycare center in Vermont. I guess I'm about 50 percent serious about it. I'm terrible at planning. I can't do long-range things very well. When the time comes, I'll do something." On religion: "I've always believed in God, but God has changed." On politics: "I got involved like everyone else in petitions and marches, then I thought it was all absurd, and I don't bother with it any more." On sexual standards: "The first time I see a person, if I want to sleep with him, something clicks—the vibrations he gives off. . . . I just trust my instincts."

Throughout her college interview, Debbie focused on her fascination with possibility, her experimentation with altering her consciousness and perceiving reality through varied lenses. She was drawn to cosmic experiences, feelings of unification with the universe that allowed her to feel that she could be whatever she wanted to be. At the same time, however, Debbie maintained a cynical view of her mystical heights and felt unable to fully commit herself to "being in the clouds."

> I always think it would be so easy if I were an artist. Then I could say, "I'm an artist and I'm driven to create this art." But I'm not. I'm just an average sort of person and—I don't know. I used to think I was mystically endowed and had cosmic consciousness. I felt that everyone could see, but I could *really* see. Everyone knew things, but I *really* knew things. Almost as if I had seen the light, and, of course, it couldn't be explained, it could just be felt.
>
> Up to a certain age, I believed everything my parents said. Then, in college, I saw all these new ideas, and I said, "OK, I'm not going to believe all that stuff you told me," and I rejected everything and said to myself, "OK, now I'm going to make a new Debbie which has nothing to do with my mother and father. I'm going to start with a clean slate," and what I started to put on it were all new ideas, and these ideas were opposite to what my parents believed. But slowly what's happening is that I'm feeling incomplete, and I realize that what's happening is that I'm adding on a lot of the things which they've told me, and I'm taking them as my own, and I'm coming more together with them.
>
> When I went to live in England, I met this woman who was very mystical. She was my men-

tor. I look at people a lot like that—like they're going to teach me something. And she took it for granted that I was equal to her, so this image I had of her—wonderful, gifted, mystical person—and she treated me as an equal, and I began to feel that I must be like her. And we were both into Eastern religion and everything is all one; it's a wonderful unified cosmos and we're all part of it and all there is [is] to love each other, and I was really feeling it. I was feeling at one with trees. I kept changing my name. I could be anything I wanted. It was all one.

Then I came back to America. It's like you can't afford to have stars in your eyes in America or any of that mystical stuff. In India, people go up in the mountains, and for years they try to reach these heightened states of consciousness. And in Berkeley, for the mere price of $149.95, you can go home and practice biofeedback—your alpha level will go right up to your potential. You just go to the seminar every Saturday and pay your money, and *you* are going to reach nirvana. It made me feel foolish to have believed what I did. I just became cynical.

You have to make up your mind. If you want to be in the clouds you can't be half-assed about it and keep one foot on the ground just in case those are only just clouds.

For awhile I just believed what I wanted to believe, and I had my own reality. Then I came back to my house, and it was, "Debbie, will you help me dust?" "Sure." And that was reality, and I couldn't sit there having vibrations. I've become cynical.

The summer before I came to college, I hung around this corner all summer. This was life to me. What did I know? Then I came to college, and there were all these people who came from all different places; and there were really rich people and smart people and freaky people and people who didn't believe in God, and there were so many things—drugs, sex, hippies. It was all very confusing.

I have no idea about the future. There are all possibilities open to me, and what it has done has totally confused me. In the old days, it was so easy. Either you were going to get married or you weren't going to get married. You were going to be a teacher or a nurse. But now you can go anywhere and do anything, and there are so many possibilities that—I don't know. I could be doing something I couldn't name because I don't know it exists yet.

Debbie described her parents as having been opposite in character. Her mother was warm, soft, and quiet, while her father was loud, aggressive, and demanding. She felt that she had elements of both in her nature. Although she described her family as having been close, she seemed to have little emotional investment in them. She recalled, at age thirteen, telling her parents that she did not need parents any more except for food and shelter. Debbie had always been involved in peer culture, and when her parents tried to impose restrictions regarding hours or friends, she fought them until they relented.

From an early time, Debbie had the sense of being special. She and her sisters were the smartest pupils in their school, and her father had great pride in and expectations of his daughters. Although Debbie always admired her mother, she felt different from her. She saw her mother as gentle, sure of herself, peaceful, and calm. In contrast, Debbie felt in herself an aggressiveness and adventurousness that never left her satisfied with herself, her friends, or her world.

For Debbie, as for the other two women in the Moratorium/Diffusion subgroup of the college Diffusions, struggle with important questions was central to her life. Although their conflicts did not focus specifically on psychosocial identity issues—at least, not the ones used to define the statuses—they were not passively resigning themselves to amorphousness. Their lives tended to be marked by movement between Moratorium and Diffusion states as they tried new modes of being, searched for answers, quested for meaning, then gave up for awhile only to begin again.

These women seemed not, however, to be involved in the separation/autonomy struggle central to Moratorium women. They had, to the contrary, rejected their parents and their life-styles without conscious conflict. They had disowned their pasts and had decided what they were not going to be. Conflict was handled largely by repression or denial. Choices tended to be the choices of parts of themselves, while the remaining parts were left to object. In this vein, Debbie spoke of feeling "incomplete." Their ideal was to be something special, but the goals they aspired to were unrealistic and did not take account of the people they had already been.

The parents of these women all seemed to have had high expectations of their daughters (particularly the fathers). Yet these expectations of greatness and specialness tended to have an amorphous tone; these women never seemed to have a concrete sense of what they were supposed to have been. This ideal, given its vagueness, also appeared to have been immune to the experiences in reality that tend to force revisions. As Debbie expressed it, they could have their own reality—at least, for a time. These women had lived a kind of double life, existing and coping in reality while maintaining a strong investment in a private world. Like Debbie, they tended to search for totalistic, romanticized experiences, where they could exist at a pinnacle of being. These experiences took them outside the social mainstream, which required too much compromise and delivered too little emotional pitch.

There was a striking developmental theme among these women in regard to their mothers. After having idealized their mothers, they discovered in latency that they were completely unlike them. They spoke of having always wished to be like their mothers, who were warm, loving, giving, and extremely talented domestically or artistically. And they felt great disappointment when they found that they did not have their mothers' gifts. Again reality did not provide what had been wished for.

Toward their fathers, these women felt intense ambivalence, and some of their inner difficulties were traceable to conflicts in this relationship. Unable to be like their mothers and wishing to be less like their fathers, these women seemed to have no other recourse besides casting around among the multitude of possibilities in the larger society for a totally new mode of being. Lacking solid and trusted internalized others against whom to test what they really were, they found their quest a difficult one.

Debbie at Thirty-Three. In the twelve years after graduating from college, Debbie followed her fantasy of going anywhere and doing anything. At present, as she looks back at herself in college, she judges herself to have been "naive." On leaving college, she felt less interested in pursuing an occupation and more bent on "living my life" or, in one of her preferred phrases, "unfolding as a person." She took several jobs where she could pursue her interest in "helping people," but these jobs did not fulfill her hopes. "I filled out form after form [as a caseworker]. Indeed, it was a job of form with no content. After three months, I quit, giving [as] my reason for leaving that the job was uninteresting and irrelevant."

Shortly thereafter, a year after college, she met and married Brett, an artist, and they began traveling the world together. Their relationship was built on intensity, often drug induced: "We met while doing LSD. That's the kind of relationship he and I had. Everything was very magical and energized and high— very all possibilities—and everything was very adventurous and open, and everything was like sparks flying and nerve ends opening and life happening [deep sigh]; and then what happened, I think, is that we both began to grow. I became tired or something, and I began to want to build my ego up again. I didn't want to be smashed into a million fragments. . . . In those days, anything intense was very real and meaningful to me. It didn't seem to matter whether the intensity was in the direction of pain or joy." For six years, this increasingly ambivalent relationship absorbed her. She found it difficult to break her vows in the marriage and felt that her husband had become her family. Interestingly, they had had a traditional church wedding with a large reception.

Debbie's marriage to Brett seems to have continued two patterns apparent at the end of college. First, it may have been an effort to unite two sides of herself—the traditional, family-rooted Debbie of domesticity and Debbie the mystical adventurer. The act of getting married and meaning it, taking it seriously, was traditional while her choice of husband was sensation seeking.

The second resonating pattern was her disillusionment with ego-shattering experiences. In her college interview, Debbie spoke poignantly of her bruising returns to reality after flights in the clouds. At this time, it seemed as though she could integrate this lesson. Yet her marriage seemed to be one more effort to reach for this peak of experience, and again her reaction was similar, to tire of it, to wish to be back on the ground.

The period of separation and divorce from Brett was painful for Debbie. Living, at the time, far from her family and former friends, Debbie resisted her parents' urging to return home and set out to "make myself anew." She deliberately took part-time jobs with little responsibility, the better to focus on an inner search for her "true self." As in college, she turned to Eastern mysticism and spent much time meditating and keeping a journal. "I was emptying myself so I could get to the core of me and my life and then re-create myself."

During this time she became close to one of Brett's friends, also an artist, but more settled, less scattered. After a somewhat longer period of being together than she had with Brett, Debbie married this new man, Bob, with whom she still feels she has excellent communication. "Although both of us are older and some of our views have tempered, we both feel it's important to remain open and questioning, and we are both trying to look at ourselves and see who we are and grow into all that we might be—perhaps." What they share, as Debbie puts it, is "being into exploring with life."

One outcome of Debbie's almost monastic inner search-

ing was a decision to enter teaching in a radical school, one focused on "guiding children to their true selves." She had, at the
time of the interview, been teaching for a year and found it satisfying, challenging, and creative, the first such work experience
she had had.

Overall, at present, Debbie gives the impression of trying
to settle into her occupational and marriage commitments. She
and Bob are trying to conceive, in order to "experience family
anew." But although she sounds more bound to reality than
previously, she remains determined to cling to her sense of possibility. To most questions related to the future, Debbie says, "I
don't know how, with what life offers me, I will react." Asked
what she would like to do in the future, she replies, "I might
write some day or become a counselor or something else I
haven't even thought of yet"—essentially the same reply she had
given in college.

This summary does not adequately capture the ragged-
ness of Debbie's life before her marriage to Bob. She had had,
for example, four abortions, many unusual relationships with
unusual people, brushes with death of those close to her.
Throughout this time, she became close again to her mother and
two sisters, although her relationship with her father has continued to be ambivalent and difficult.

The vagueness and fluidity about Debbie are saved by her
almost poetic expression of her acute perceptions. Her commitments are to experience itself. Everything, however, is elevated
to a high plane; she takes nothing for granted. She is still fascinated with merger, with the wish to lose herself in another,
which she did for a time with Brett and is probably also doing
with Bob, but less so. But, having merged, she then needs to
withdraw and regroup, redraw her boundaries. The paradox of
Debbie is that all the indefiniteness of herself, the search for
other states of consciousness, the energy of playing with her
own mind exist in the context of some fundamental strength
that keeps her together at the same time that she is going over
the edge. Although Debbie defines herself by her internal focus, she is most connected to reality by her relationships with

others. It is as though, lacking inner structure, she reaches out to others for the pieces she is missing.

It is impossible to predict the success of Debbie's current commitments; they are too new and she is too impulsive and volatile. One sees her struggle—a continuation of the college struggle—to find firm ground on which to stake herself without betraying other aspects of her self, without foreclosing possibility, change, and growth. Unlike the other still-diffuse Diffusions discussed earlier, Debbie has an internal focus. It is not an insightful one, but she does experiment with her own malleability. In contrast to Susan, for example, who picks herself up after getting knocked down by life, Debbie tries to understand her life, to find its meaning by looking inward.

Settled and Committed

Three of the Diffusion women have made commitments and are, at present, leading lives with clearly defined goals. They have, however, embraced their choices totalistically, without ambivalence or struggle, and all these choices rest on an external agent. Of the three who will be discussed, two were judged to be Foreclosed Diffusions at the end of college. One, like Debbie, was a Moratorium Diffusion but followed a course different from Debbie.

Evelyn

In her college interview, Evelyn was covered with open psychological wounds, living perilously close to raw and painful feelings. She was emerging from a serious depression, for which she was in psychotherapy, and was in retreat from her involvement in the drug culture. Desperately low in self-esteem, Evelyn had tried fruitlessly to win the love and approval of her distant, critical father, whom she adored. She had grown up in the shadow of a gifted older sister, whom she idealized. Her mother had been largely emotionally unavailable when she needed her. Evelyn was so deeply in the throes of working through old family conflicts and disappointments that she was not much able to participate in the expansive aspects of college. Rebellious and angry, she was involved in pointless sexual experiences and drug-induced emotional states, mysticism, and philosophical questions.

She had no idea what she wanted to do with her life or what she believed in but seemed, at the time of the interview, to be trying to get herself organized. "I dropped out of school after sophomore year. I was sick of studying and went to work, and that was so awful I went back to school. And then I got into drugs until one day when I had a really bad trip and my whole self-image shattered; I realized I wasn't what I thought I was. I realized I was really alone and had never really let anyone know me. I had had an image of myself as a strong-willed individual who did everything correctly. And there I was—a terrified little girl. So I stopped drugs and started therapy I was brought up to think you don't have problems, and I'm just starting now to confront some of them."

It was quite a different person who came to be interviewed twelve years later. This Evelyn, although she vaguely remembered me, was guarded and distant, took a long time to relax and talk freely. Her wounds had healed and her feelings had submerged. In contrast to her college experience, she was leading a constricted and narrowed life and doing it with apparent contentment.

After graduation from college, Evelyn decided to take whatever job was highest paying, which turned out to be a responsible clerical job in the corporation where her mother had a secretarial job. She has been with the company ever since, moving up through the ranks with increasing administrative responsibility. This job hierarchy has provided a structure around which to organize herself, as she plots each new promotion, studies the politics, and increases her skills. "Upward mobility," as she puts it, is what is central in her life. Her political views have grown conservative, but she has involved herself in local issues and has strong opinions about national and world events. She reads a great deal and generally feels connected to society.

Evelyn had a disappointing love affair with a man she met

shortly before graduating from college. They were involved for five years, but he abruptly broke off the relationship when they were unable to reconcile their differing views of marriage. She came away feeling deeply and personally rejected. Since then, Evelyn has not found anyone to care about as seriously. She is philosophical about the possibility of marriage. "If it happens, it happens," but she seems not to fret about it and is not actively looking for someone.

Her father having died four years ago, Evelyn's mother has come to live with her. Her mother has become her best friend, and they share a mutual and close relationship. The rest of Evelyn's time is focused on caring for her house—which she owns and has learned to repair herself—on activities with companions (who are clearly more companions than friends), and on a number of mainly solitary hobbies and interests.

In response to a question about the main good experiences of the past ten years, Evelyn focused on things she owns and is proud of owning. Bad experiences involve her losses in relationships—her boyfriend and her father. Her hopes for the future center on additional things she would like to have.

Evelyn appears to have closed off much that had been in turmoil during college, as though it had threatened to overwhelm her and she decided it was better buried. She dismisses these experiences as a bad time and, in retrospect, does not feel her therapy was helpful (she remained in therapy only a few months). "I had to do it on my own," she says.

At present, Evelyn does not appear to be depressed. Looking over the past twelve years, Evelyn is proud of "getting to be the person that I am, getting as far as I have in my job. It wasn't easy, and I did that on my own. I don't think I'm doing that badly."

This last statement seems to be the best summary of her psychological state. The shadow of her crisis experience seems to remain with her. She had touched bottom and has now reorganized in quite a different direction. Remembering her turmoil, she can be pleased with the tranquility she has achieved and does not ask more of life.

Evelyn had been in a Moratorium/Diffusion state during

college and has developed a basically Foreclosure pattern of identity. Although her path is an unusual one, she has much in common with the now-committed women who had been Foreclosed Diffusions during college.

Darlene

Darlene was raised on the West Coast, and her parents were both highly educated and socially prominent. They were intellectuals who discussed everything and believed in nothing. Because her parents were involved in a variety of social and professional activities, she thought she might like to go back to the West Coast after college and find something to do.

Religiously, Darlene's parents were "very open" and never raised her any particular way. She believed in "some kind of Being which could fit any religion" but felt that she, like her father, had more questions than answers. Her political convictions were similar.

With respect to sex, Darlene denied that it could in any way be a moral issue, feeling that what was important was a person's emotions. As a result, she had no set standards and did what "feels right." Her parents had discussed sex with her quite a bit; their views were that one should have a "relationship" prior to sexual involvement. To Darlene, their view implied a certain cautiousness that she could not manage in her own behavior, but she admitted to not being sure what was meant by a "relationship." For example, Darlene said that the previous week she had had intercourse with a casual friend "because I had kissed him, and if I went that far. . . ." When she thought about this behavior later, she had some initial doubts about her action, then decided that because she had done it, it must have been right at the time, and if it was right at the time, then it must still be right. Her father had warned her that people can get "screwed up" by sex. Darlene felt that it was important not to be screwed up by sex, so she never allowed herself to feel any conflict about these matters.

Darlene was rooted in the present, wished to forget the past, and was unable to envision a future. Always active in causes and groups and with her friends, she seemed to have gained momentary pleasure from these activities, but none had a lasting effect. Darlene was quite vague about her history. The interviewer felt that she truly could not remember very much rather than that she was being evasive. She had few friends when young, preferring the company of her family and their friends. Much of this period of her life focused on social appearances, and she was, like her family, most concerned with being at the "right" places with the "right" people. These social pleasantries had a faddishness about them; something new was always "in."

One sensed an emotional emptiness both in Darlene and in her recounting of her life. Her relationships seemed stereotyped and distant. One of her dreams suggested her sense of being an observer in life as well as her deep, unconscious fear of being abandoned: "It was a huge coliseum, filled up with all the people I've known in my life. And there was a big dinner. My boyfriend was with me, and my parents were there. There was a wedding ceremony going on. It was very proper, waltz-type dancing. There were trapezes all over the place, but everyone was waltzing. My boyfriend was dancing, and I was sitting on the side lines, and I felt he was leaving me completely alone."

At the end of college, Darlene and others who were Foreclosed Diffusions seemed to experience themselves as leaves waiting for a gust of wind. They suffered from atrophy of the will, acting for the moment, unable to define a consistent direction.

After college, as she had mentioned in her interview, Darlene did return home to see what there was for her to do. Her mother found her a job in an agency where she began to do social service work. She enrolled for further training in social work, although she never completed a degree, and began specializing in group work. Because of many moves around the country, Darlene has held a variety of jobs. She says, "My strength is in enabling others to become more whole, and I, too, benefit from such facilitating relationships."

Darlene spent the first five postcollege years involved with a man with whom she ultimately broke off. A month after, she met the husband she married two months later. She describes her husband as being much like her father, both in the same profession. And Darlene is in an occupation much like her mother's. She now has two young children, who are her first priority. Although she has temporarily suspended her career, doing only occasional volunteer projects, she maintains her interest and enthusiasm for working and intends to return to active involvement as soon as the children need her less.

Despite the fact that Darlene has been creative and effective in her work, having written one book and planning a second, she has organized her life around her husband's career. A number of times, she made geographical moves because of his advancement but expressed no resentment. She does, however, feel burdened by the constant demands of her children and longs for time to herself. It is not clear why she has forgone her career for her family to such an extent; perhaps it is because she feels that she is expected to. The center of Darlene's life is her relationships with others, especially her husband and children. Her work is also people-oriented, and she enjoys the opportunity to discuss personally relevant issues.

Darlene expresses great joy and pride in how well she and her husband have managed their lives. They have made some difficult transitions but have moved smoothly. One of the most effusively happy women in the whole sample, Darlene seems delighted with all aspects of her life, except for her complaints about feeling too tied down to the children. But even her complaints have a good-natured quality. Of both her children and her parents, she says, "I think we have quite an extraordinary family." She admires and respects her parents, still feels close to them. She continues to have an intensely loving relationship with her husband. She has many friends.

On one level, Darlene seems quite healthy, focused and settled but still alive and growing. She is attempting to find creative solutions to the career/family conflict while deliberately choosing to give priority to the family. But Darlene's picture of her life has something of the quality of protesting too much; everything is *very* rosy.

Darlene is clearly more integrated than she was in college; the fortuitous first job gave her a feeling of success and

helped her build a career commitment. The romanticized, idealized relationship to her husband gave structure to the rest of her
life. It is evident, from a distance, however, that Darlene has
re-created in her own life the life of her parents. She and her
husband are doing the same things that her mother and father
did. In values and ideals, they are identical. She is not consciously aware of this similarity, but she says that she sees herself as "very much the product of my family." In this sense,
Darlene, like Evelyn, has gone home again. College, for them,
was a period of experimentation, but their lives have followed
the threads of their precollege selves.

Gretchen

Much like Darlene in her college interview, Gretchen had
also been grouped as a Foreclosed Diffusion, embedded in her
family network, uncertain of her own goals or beliefs, but organizing herself via a relationship with her boyfriend. Gretchen
took her first job based on where her boyfriend was located and
soon discovered in herself a talent for photography. Her boyfriend became her husband, but she continued to pursue and
succeed at her photographic work. Giving priority to her career, she was working in a different city from her husband, although they maintained a commuter relationship. During this
time, however, both became involved in extramarital sexual relationships and considerable drug experimentation. Close to
divorce, they together became "reborn" through involvement in
an Eastern religious sect. Gretchen, on advice from her spiritual
leader, took up residence with her husband, and they together
began to live out a life of spirituality and meditation. They now
have three children, but Gretchen is pursuing her photography
part of the time. Most of the decisions in Gretchen's life, including a requirement of sexual abstinence, are now made by
her spiritual leader. He, rather than her husband, is the most important person in her life. She feels that she has found the
"true path" and has organized her life around it. .
    In Gretchen, we see another form of Foreclosure, this
time not on aspects of her family of origin but in a totalistic

system that answers all her questions and to which she can adjust in toto. In spite of her fortunate discovery of a talent that led to a successful career, Gretchen had been unable to organize the rest of her life. Her lack of inner structure was exacting its price. It seems that Gretchen was in need of external discipline and, once it was provided, was able to settle into a goal-oriented, if constricted, way of life.

Diffusions as a Group

The Identity Diffusions all experience failures in internalization, the taking in of aspects of relationship and experience that come to be seen as part of the self. Experience occurs but does not produce learning or change. Nor is the self enriched. As a result, personality does not become structured, and the woman remains like a Pirandello character, ready to respond as the situation demands. She can act on impulse but without a basis for determining whether the expression of the impulse makes sense for her. Being this or that, believing this or that, it's all the same. When one begins with little inner attachment to a conception of the self, one does not demand consistency from later experiences. Because inner experiences do not fit together with other inner experiences, the sense of one's self fluctuates wildly. In states of Identity Diffusion, there is no inner demand to integrate these experiences or to make sense of them or to connect them. Little is rejected as "not me," so anything becomes possible. As a result, the self remains at the mercy of impulse and environmental forces. This underlying personality fragmentation is common to both the still-diffuse and the now-committed Diffusions.

Those who have made commitments are those who allowed themselves to be "claimed." Evelyn, Darlene, and Gretchen, each in somewhat different ways, are using external agents to organize themselves internally. They each accept narrowing and limits as a way of controlling the impulsivity and confusion beneath the surface. They have learned the dangers of trusting oneself or following an inner direction and have found themselves benign jailers.

Although the committed Diffusions profess to be satisfied with their lives and are, indeed, a great deal more optimistic and emotionally balanced than they were at the end of college, one wonders whether they have paid too high a price. Evelyn and Gretchen are achieving in the work world, and we can well expect Darlene to achieve again. Both Gretchen and Darlene are experiencing their generativity, having settled, for better in Darlene's case, for worse in Gretchen's, the intimacy tasks. Yet one senses aspects of these women that are being kept suppressed. One wonders how their children will experience them as mothers.

Several of this group of women have spoken of their interest in helping others to be whole, an externalized effort, perhaps, to repair their own sense of fragmentation. Except for Debbie, none of these women can think clearly about how they wish to grow as a person, although many have plans for what they wish to do. Debbie thinks about who she is as a person but not clearly. The solution to the Diffusion dilemma, then, seems to be not to solve it. Get something (a job or a religion) or someone (a husband) to tell you how to live your life and accept that authority. This solution allows one to function but does not seem to lead to ego development.

Erikson (1968) discusses the propensity for "totalistic" solutions to be found, especially among Identity Diffuse adolescents. He traces this propensity to superego pathology, specifically, a superego that remains infantile and primitive in its "categoric" attitude. One aspect common to these women as they appeared in college was their general effort to disavow the superego, reflecting their incapacity to modify or integrate its functions. The committed Diffusions are women who have made peace with the superego by accepting its demands for total "goodness." As a result, they suffer neither ambivalence nor guilt. Perhaps this lack of moral ambiguity, of superego tension, is what makes them seem so static.

The still-diffuse Diffusions are, in a sense, in search of the organizing principles that the others have found. They are people looking for an authority. Susan is trying to do what Gretchen has done, embrace religion. Debbie is trying to make experience itself an organizing principle. Why the still-diffuse Diffusions have not been able to find such authority thus far remains a puzzle. They are perhaps somewhat more fragmented than the others, have fewer Foreclosing possibilities open to them. But this path cannot be predicted from the early data.

One is tempted to suggest that the general upheaval in the roles of women contributed to the difficulty of these women in smoothly identifying with clear modes of being. Erikson views the lack of well-defined rituals and passages as a strain on a weak ego attempting to formulate an identity. These women grew into womanhood at the height of the turmoil in the women's movement. But, if they were affected by it, it was not consciously. Sex-role conflicts seem to be an individual, rather than a socially determined, area of concern for these women.

The social forces that most strongly color their lives are the ones that make anything possible. The lack of social taboos, the sense of "anything goes" are social phenomena that did seem to increase the pressure, by expanding the choices, on the ego capacities of these women. Having largely escaped parental influence by the conclusion of college, they no longer had to please parents or conform to the standards with which they were raised. Moves far from home are commonplace among this group, thereby making it possible for someone like Debbie to re-create herself far from a self that was known and recognized as a self with a history. Gretchen was able to experiment with a commuter marriage, with social approbation, but was unable to control herself in the absence of spousal restraint. Susan found social support for having a baby without a husband or income, while Evelyn lives a highly independent, nonintimate life without criticism from others.

The social freedom of the past ten years has required inner structuralization from these women. Decrease in restriction, increase in freedom are factors that make identity formation a harder task. The "successful" Diffusions seem to be the ones who have found the social anchors to, in Fromm's (1941) phrase, escape from these freedoms.

Clearly these data show that Identity Diffusion in college is not a transitory state and should be taken seriously as a signal of an ego in distress. Several women in this group (Evelyn in college, Susan after the death of her child, Debbie when her marriage was breaking up, and another still-diffuse woman) have had brief encounters with psychotherapy. Each time the therapy was apparently directed to the presenting symptom or crisis and did not attempt to address the underlying ego structure.

Most of these women, reflecting on their college experience, express the regret that they were not more focused than they were or that they did not take their studies or occupational planning more seriously than they did. All, except Evelyn, found the college years to be stimulating and expanding, and stress the new possibilities that were opened to them. As we have seen, however, these Diffusion women, because of their personality structure, were not much able to make use of these possibilities or of the opportunity for psychosocial growth. Either they became overwhelmed by the options, lost in the sea of choice after having severed their moorings, or else they swam to a safe shore to avoid drowning.

We have no good theoretical yardsticks by which to measure these lives. All these Diffusion women have found ways of functioning that reflect reasonable if not optimal mental health. Yet one wonders whether they could not have, with good psychotherapeutic intervention, formed flexible and freely chosen identities.

For half the women who were Diffusions in college, identity is no longer a central concern. Their lives are oriented to implementing the choices they have made. For the other half, ten to twelve years later, identity formation remains an as-yet-unsolved life task, and they appear to be as far from settling these issues as they were in college.

Chapter 8

Conclusion:
Reflections on
Female Identity

"Do you know who made you?" "Nobody, as I
knows on," said the child, with a short laugh. . . .
"I 'spect I grow'd."
  —*Harriet Beecher Stowe, Uncle Tom's Cabin*

The configuration of a woman's identity at the close of adolescence forms the template for her adulthood. Knowing about the
structural basis of a woman's identity tells us a great deal more
about her psychology than knowing about the specific choices
she makes. If we know a woman's identity status at the end of
college, we can predict reasonably well the course of her early
adulthood, which, we may suppose, will in turn predict her middle adulthood. In each of the four identity statuses are married
women, single women, married women with children, women
with serious careers, and women who are full-time homemakers.
Yet the identity statuses are internally coherent as groups and
demarcate different pathways women traverse on their way to
identity formulations.

Women characterized as Foreclosures, Identity Achievements, or Diffusions at the end of college are likely to remain
so, although women who are Diffuse in identity may, through

luck, find a benevolent organizing force. Identity Achievements and Moratoriums are capable of more original and individualized choices, forging creative modes of living that are open to surprise and change. The Moratorium status during college is an unstable one. Such women take the greatest risks in trying to make of themselves something quite different from what they had been. Because they have swum so far from shore, they are the most vulnerable; and some, frightened by the currents, merely swim home again.

For this age cohort of women, a plethora of possibility was open. As a result, we might have expected their identity formation to reside in the choice among and the integration of many potential identities. Instead, we find a choice between the pulls of the past and relatively narrow options for the future. The world entered by the adolescent girl at the dawn of adulthood is not the exotic, unusual one of our theories but a world that has been familiar to the individual all along. It is striking, for example, how many of these women found their first jobs through people they knew or how many met their husbands through mutual friends. Women move along in the world through relational connections: Whom they know has much to do with whom—and how—they become.

Separation-Individuation in Women

Throughout the lives of these women, irrespective of their identity-status grouping, runs the theme of distance from home. In forging their identities, some women have psychologically never left home (the Foreclosures), some have gone home again, and some have gone on to independent, unique ways of being that they may or may not bring home. Developmental differences among the women in the four identity-status groups seem to rest on the continuum of separation-individuation, and the identities of these women reflect the degree to which separation-individuation has been undertaken and accomplished.

In that the theory of separation-individuation has been written largely with men in mind, we must proceed cautiously to understand this process in women. The notion of a separate identity or a separate sense of self is not quite the same in women as in men.

Chodorow (1978) has demonstrated that women never separate or individuate as much as men because of their early developmental history. Because mothers and daughters are of the same gender, according to Chodorow, the daughter's primary love object is the same as the person with whom she identifies. While the boy must pull himself away from his primary attachment to mother in order to identify himself as a male with father, the girl has no need of such drastic separation. She identifies with the first person she loves. As a result, girls experience themselves as being more continuous with others, not having to erect the barriers of differentiation and separateness that boys do. Boundaries of the self are never as rigid in girls as in boys, and the basic female sense of self is connected, with a good deal of fluidity, to the world. This developmental fact of continuity with others explains, in part, girls' greater capacity for empathy and their greater preoccupation with relationships with others.

Because the daughter is of the same gender as her mother, a mother's primary investment in her daughter, who is always to some extent a narcissistic extension of herself, is likely to last longer and to be more intense than her relation to a son. Separation between mothers and daughters then is only partial; at some level they always remain emotionally bound up with each other as though neither ever quite sees herself as a fully separate person.

In adolescence, the struggle to get further away from mother, to further individuate, recurs. But separation is made difficult by years of intense attachment. Although girls move toward genital heterosexuality, they retain an internal emotional triangle, never fully giving up their attachment to their primary emotional caretaker, their mother. Their experience of self as intertwined with the world continues, playing itself out in a widening circle of relationships. Loving, feeling at one with, and being like are then part of an undisrupted process rooted in the early relationship between a girl and her mother (Chodorow, 1978).

In a study of 3,000 adolescents, Douvan and Adelson (1966) were surprised to find how pervasive the differences were between the boys and the girls. The overwhelming interpersonal focus of the girls stood in sharp relief against the push for autonomy among the boys. For the girls, it seemed, identity was a matter of defining the internal experience of the self through attachments to others. Gilligan (1982) similarly concluded that the concept of identity must be widened for women to include the experience of interconnection.

Many writers have posited two main threads of human experience. One line includes self-assertion, mastery, individual distinction, and separateness; the other includes the need for contact, union, cooperation, and being together. Bakan (1966) called these two basic lines *agency* and *communion*. If we think of psychological development taking place along these two lines, we notice that separation-individuation has been conceptualized only along agentic lines—that is, we think of development as leading toward increasing separateness and selfhood. But for women the agentic story is only part of the tale and the less crucial part at that. As we have seen, the critical issues for the women of this study have seldom been agentic ones. Communion is central to female development, and women are likely to opt for preserving attachment before pursuing their agentic needs. For many women, success in communion, in relationship, is itself an expression of agentic needs for assertion and mastery.

The problem of separating is the problem of not only becoming different but of becoming different and maintaining connection at the same time. To the little girl, being liked means being like. Attachment implies sameness. "I love my mother and want to grow up to be just like her" is the hallmark of identification processes in the little girl. With becoming like mother and therefore pleasing her comes the assurance of remaining forever attached to her.

To be different yet attached is one of the great challenges of human relatedness. Difference implies dispute; it implies that one is good and the other bad, especially at lower levels of developmental maturity. For the developing girl, being rooted in the family, most often mother, is a secure position of selfhood.

When she expresses family values and priorities, she knows that she is good in the eyes of those who matter most to her. Therefore, she can value herself. Difference may invoke disapproval or, at least, the fantasy of disapproval. The teenage girl, although increasingly aware of options and possibilities, does not greet these choices as choices for herself: Other people may become different, but that is not "our" way. To be distinct is to eschew the "we," and that is painful.

Among the women whose lives we have considered here, the watershed issues of identity tend not to be political or occupational but social and religious. They internalize the central priorities of their mothers as the issues to feel the same or different about. As college-age, late adolescents, these women judge their distance from their families by whether and how much they carry on family religious traditions, whom they choose as friends, what sexual values they adopt, how they dress, whether and when and whom they plan to marry. These are the pivotal points of negotiation in the separation-individuation drama.

Girls who try to decide these matters on their own terms most often search out a boyfriend to help leverage them out of the family nexus. What is striking about these relationships, when we view them deeply, is that they are seldom romantic ones. Rather, the boyfriend has meaning as a surrogate parent and is usually just as controlling. Again the issues revolve around the central priorities—how to act, how much and when to study, how to dress, how much personal freedom she may have. When we interview young women who have passed out of the early college-age preoccupation with what their parents expect and want of them, they are most likely to be centered on what their boyfriends expect and want of them. Often, they accept their boyfriends' authority gladly, as they once accepted their parents'. The battle being waged here is the struggle of sameness, where partners try to coerce the other into being like them. "If you are like me, I like you. If you like me, you'd better be like me." The discussion is not about power but about attachment. And, again, attachment and sameness are confounded, much as they were, as Chodorow points out, in the earliest mother/daughter bond.

It is startling that so many of these women in early adulthood perceive themselves as very much like their mothers when they seem, at least from an objective perspective, to be so different. For one thing, most of them are combining work and childrearing while their mothers did not. This difference, however, appears to be less important—at least to the women themselves—than might have been supposed. These women seem to be saying that they remain like mother in the important ways, in the ways that they valued her for; they are nurturant, family-oriented, loving toward others. That they have careers too does not make them different from mother, just busier. They see themselves as trying to raise their children in ways similar to the way they were raised, to re-create the home that their mothers provided them.

The quality of identification with mother and her persisting importance exists in these women largely as a sense of seeing things through mother's eyes, a sense that is intermittently but consistently present. The internal presence of mother, her wishes and her approving smile, hovers just at the corner of consciousness, an ever-present other to whom a woman is continually responding. The young woman may experience this presence as only a fleeting sense that "my mother would like that" or "my mother would not approve of this." This maternal *Doppelgänger,* however it is experienced and construed, bounds and limits the choices a woman may make. To some extent, a woman is destined to realize some essence of her mother, whether it be in domesticity, nurturance, dress, or values. Not to integrate part of the mother brings the risk of Identity Diffusion; some aspect of mother must be mixed in the identity in order to bind it, to make it cohere.

To ensure this continuity, 85 percent of the women in this study remain close to their mothers, nearly half choosing her as the person they feel closest or second closest to in the world. (In contrast, 48 percent remain close to their fathers; only two women chose him as the first or second closest person to them.) Many phone or see their mothers every day, ask their mothers' advice on matters big and small, or, if not in need of advice, they at least include their mothers in the decision-making process. This finding may be shocking to those whose impressions of contemporary women are gleaned from reading the psychological literature or the popular press. As these sources have it, women today have left their mothers behind in the dust, regard them as old-fashioned, or disregard them altogether. These women, however, ordinary and unremarkable as they may be, report that mother is a central source of emotional as well as logistical support.

In this regard, the Moratoriums provide the most interesting example. Having struggled against their mother's example and control during their late adolescence, they are most likely of all four groups to feel close to her as early adults. Going home again for this group seems to mean a return to a psychological place where they can once again feel intensely connected to their mothers. The Identity Achievements, by contrast, are least likely to remain intensely close to their mothers. Their struggles with mother during adolescence were, in general, less intense and dramatic than those of the Moratoriums and less guilt-ridden as a result. The Achievements, then, gradually achieve psychological distance from mother, generally using boyfriends/husbands or career involvement to connect themselves to a new anchor.

Anchoring

Anchoring is perhaps the best metaphorical word to describe the communion aspect of the separation-individuation process after late adolescence. It stands to reason that if something is separated from, something else must be found to replace it. Similarly, that which is individuated must be reworked into something new.

The Moratorium phase is one of casting off the anchor lines. College presents a number of new possibilities to which to attach: relationships, causes, or career goals. Moratoriums in college were primarily searching for new friends and new groups that might accept them. The end of college brought a dispersal of this new community however, so that those who remained Moratoriums were cut adrift. Some, like Millie, cast about for a while, trying to find something to reattach to; others, like Marlene, clung desperately to a boyfriend from the college years and followed him. Still others, like Meredith, simply found the larger world too cold and threatening and quickly returned home, physically and psychologically. Those Moratoriums who went on to achieve identities, as well as most of the Identity Achievements, are women who found a new anchor point that provided a transition between college and the rest of their lives.

The process of anchoring is critical to identity formation in women because the self is experienced so much in relation to others. Who a woman is reflects her sense of what she means to others. This process is not at all passive because, as Erikson points out, a person can choose those people she wishes to have meaning to.

Anchoring seems to take place in one of four areas for the women we have been observing: primary family, husband/children, career, friends—or some combination of these. Women who have anchored in their primary families choose to become purveyors of the heritage, the essence of the Foreclosure solution. Their lives feel meaningful and right because they are carrying on traditions that had made them feel secure as children and continue to be a source of comfort and belief. They express their embeddedness in their primary families by carrying on their values and customs into the next family and maintain an enviable sense of certitude that theirs is the right way to live. For women who organize themselves as Foreclosures, the prospect of not marrying is unsettling because it interrupts the pervasive life plan. Without a new family in which to carry forth the family centeredness that gives meaning to life, these women have little possibility of sending down new roots to grow from the old. Foreclosures are likely to choose husbands based on the men's likelihood of meshing with the Foreclosures' family-oriented values. They often mention liking their husband's family or his similar background as important reasons for choosing him.

The second possibility, anchoring in husband/children separate from the primary family, is a pattern found mainly among those who become Identity Achievements. Their sense of identity resides in having forged new, nonfamilially based modes of relating to others, and they have husbands who support their talents and interests. If these women work, their work is secondary. They are equally likely to define themselves by their avocational interests, crafts, sports, or leisure-time pursuits. They are intensely interested in planning and decorating their houses, in developing couple friendships. They take an active and creative interest in their children's development if they have children and think through parental choices rather than reflexively responding as their parents did. The relational web, with their new family as the center, is the anchor.

Centrality of career, a third possibility, is an anchor point for only a few women in this sample despite the fact that many have advanced degrees and all but a few are employed full-time. Although they have discovered that they are capable of accomplishing productive work in a nondomestic sphere, most of these women experience their job-related selves as secondary (and often expendable) aspects of their identities.

Those who *have* made their careers an important anchor point have typically had mentors. Anchoring in work seems not to take place unless an important other takes a personal interest in a woman's career. Only those women who obtained graduate professional degrees or who apprenticed in crafts experienced a mentoring relationship. The mentor seems to provide an entree into the field and a possibility of bonding with it in a personal way. When women have someone with recognition in their chosen field care about them, believe in them, and encourage them, they can feel a part of this new professional community and have a designated place in it by virtue of their attachment to their mentor.

The absence of mentors has dire consequences for a woman's investment in her career. Those women without mentors work, but they are not bonded to their careers in an identity-forming way. In many occupations people do their jobs without coming to feel part of a larger group with a sense of shared mission. Although there may be emotional gratifications from teaching well, for example, and from relating to young students, and although teaching may be a way of earning a livelihood, the experience of such work will not become an anchoring part of the sense of self unless there is external recognition by important others in the field. Similarly, those women engaged in the business world become interested in power and money but at a distance from the core of themselves. They do not derive meaning from their work unless, again, some important other cheers them on and models for them how meaning in work might be obtained.

Because women are so unlikely to find mentors, husbands often fill in to play this role. Much has been written about husbands who do not support their wives' occupational interests, but little has been said about husbands who aid their wives in finding meaning in work. One woman, for example, a teacher married to a principal, has a personal and vital sense of the work part of herself because of her husband's encouragement of and enthusiasm about her creative efforts in her job. Another husband both financially supports and critically engages with his wife's efforts to be a writer. He is always her first audience.

For a woman to anchor herself importantly in work, her work has to matter to someone who matters to her. When it does not, her occupational pursuits tend to be transitory as she searches for something else that will give her life meaning. The presence of even one person who validates the meaningfulness of her work can change an identity-distant job into an enriching and anchoring aspect of a woman's existence.

Disillusionment with work is a recurring theme among these women, a phenomenon that has frequently driven a talented woman back to familial sources of satisfaction. Many had had career goals centered on helping others, an ideal that paled in the face of bureaucratic and socioeconomic realities. The wish to be helpful to others, many discovered, is more likely to be realized at home than at work.

The final anchoring possibility, friendship, seems to be the one chosen when the others have been rejected or are unattainable. This is not to suggest that friendship is unimportant in women's lives. Most of these women say that their friendships with other women have been vitally important, but they are not anchors for most of them. Friendships appear to be important secondary anchors and come in two kinds. Long-term friends are people who can be counted on in any emergency. Women feel that their old friends are people who will always be there for them, who provide distant anchoring, protection from having to be all alone in the world. Recent friends provide day-to-day help with logistics and are a source of emotional support. They are companions and people to discuss problems with. Married women with children report that they do not have enough time for friendship and miss this aspect of their lives. Friendships also attach women to new aspects of the larger world that then may become woven into their identities. Friends bring with them different interests, hobbies, and ideologies that serve the continuing refinement and differentiation of identity.

Anchoring is a way of attaching to aspects of the adult world, of having a berth in it. For women, this attachment to the world involves connection to other people, even in the world of work. Anchoring for women is like a rapprochement process, where elements of the outside world are brought back to or through an important other to be integrated and made part of the self. Rarely among these women do we find an activity that brings gratification outside of an important relationship. Few women jog alone; those who do report their achievements to or share their experiences with someone else. Meaning and identity reside in connectedness.

Identity is an amalgamation and integration of these anchor points. When these women speak of what is most meaningful to them, they all tend to use the same phrase: He or she or it is "there." Or they speak of knowing that someone is "always there." Psychologically, this phrase seems to reflect the sum of those things that can be taken for granted. A sense that a person is "there for me" means that he or she can be expected to try to meet my needs. Someone who is "there" assures a woman of being the object of devotion and attention. When a career is "there," a woman is certain of skills that she can use and that will be recognized and appreciated by others.

The Web of Relatedness

The resultant sense of identity in women—the product of these anchors and webs—is a multifaceted synthesis of multiple investments, each important in its own way, each in a certain balance with the others. Once formulated, identity is edited and modified, but its central core, like a reliable clock, keeps the system functioning. It is only with great difficulty and turmoil that these central aspects of identity can later be opened to question or reworked.

While crises in occupational aspirations often produce nodal growth crises for men (Vaillant, 1977; Levinson and others, 1978), crises in relationships form such a watershed for women. As college seniors, the women in this study shared a common fantasy of the future: They would find men whom they would love and who would love them and with them they would create or, perhaps, re-create an ideal of family happiness that would someday include children. Many of these adolescent women, as we have seen, also had strong career ambitions or, at least, a wish to be productive and employed outside the home for some portion of their adult life. But, at root, they shared the idea that the central structure of their life would be a new family to absorb their emotional energy.

Those women who found a partner sooner or later in their twenties tended to intertwine their continuing psychological development (or lack of development) around this keystone relationship. They finished defining themselves in juxtaposition to the person with whom they planned to spend their life. They balanced their needs and interests against the backdrop of an important other whose attitudes and preferences were weighed in the decision making. In many ways it is easier—and, at least for a time, feels comforting—to lose oneself in someone else. Finding oneself is hard work, fraught with the anxieties of loneliness and failure. The more she feels cherished by someone she loves, the less need a woman has to wrestle with questions of her self-worth. The more she has committed herself to the welfare of another, the less need she has to ponder the expression of her own deeper self. A woman who loves makes the needs and wishes of those she loves a part of her own identity.

It is not surprising, then, that the most dramatic examples of growth and change within this sample of women are found among those whose first committed relationships ended badly. Both Alice and Marlene had to seriously rework their place in the world under the stress of losing an important relationship. The only Foreclosure who showed signs of internal growth was the one whose marriage was painfully disappointing and ended in divorce.

Losing a relationship represents more than losing a loved person. It is, more deeply, loss of a precious fantasy, the belief that someone else will be there to perform psychological functions, to soothe distress, to structure time, to stabilize and to reassure, to make one feel worthwhile. Having to learn to take over these functions for oneself seems to be growth promoting for women. Here, growth refers to increased internalization, increased ability to stand alone, to set individual goals, to be aware of who one is.

Lest it seem that I am taking the position that marriage hinders growth, let me state that those women who are leading fully interdependent lives are no less psychologically healthy and are, in many cases, more content, more anchored than those who are not. But they have, by and large, done less exploration with the self, are less sharply defined.

What, then, do we learn about the role of relationships in women's lives? Clearly, that it is not so much the having or not having of a primary relationship that counts but how the relationship is used for inner psychological functioning. For many women, especially those who are or become Foreclosures, the main function of a primary relationship with a man is the satisfaction of dependency needs. The woman wants a man to take care of her, to love her as her parents did, unconditionally and eternally. She looks to her marriage for the security she assumes she can never find within herself. Threats to the marriage are likely to throw her into a panicky state because the internal foundation of her existence is put at risk. Such a woman takes it on faith that someone has to "always be there" for her, and she is unable to imagine living on her own, drawing on her own resources. Given a satisfactory relationship, such women do quite well, expressing themselves genuinely and productively in work and in other activities. But we might worry about the long-term success of this strategy: How will they confront widowhood, for example? Or are these women building reserves of psychological strength along the way, ready to put them to use should the necessity arise?

This security-based use of relationship differs dramatically from the pattern more typical of the Achievements, which is to use relationships for self-validation and support. Here, the woman feels more whole and differentiated within herself and connects that more-defined self to another. She wants to be cared about rather than cared for. She looks to others to encourage her and reassure her but knows she must take care of herself, at least somewhat. Within the context of a primary relationship, she is likely to take more risks, experiment more freely with her attributes and capacities, and to shape the relationship to meet her unique needs. These women are also more able than the Foreclosures to acknowledge and respond to the individuality of their partners, more able to allow them to experience and express themselves. They are less threatened by change.

Superficially, these two different types of relationships may look alike. But they are experienced very differently and are rooted in quite distinct aspects of psychological development. How much or how little a woman believes, deeply believes, that she is able to take care of herself emotionally has dramatic consequences for her identity formation.

Openness to Growth and Change

Most of the women discussed here are not psychologically minded or introspective. Many of them tend to be, in Moriarty and Toussieng's (1976) distinction, censors rather than sensers. That is, they spend little energy asking themselves how they feel or trying to understand themselves psychologically. They tend to orient themselves toward keeping things running harmoniously rather than toward amplifying contradictory emotional states. Most of them report being quite happy and are content with quite ordinary happinesses. A loyal husband, a job that brings them some satisfaction, joy in children—they demand little more of life.

It may be that the ability to think and act fully independently, based on expression of one's fundamental real self, is a rare phenomenon, although an ideal to which all developmental psychologists pay homage. The need for authority is ubiquitous in adult life, as adults, no less than children, need revered others to certify their lives and sanction their choices. There are few pathfinders in this study as there exist few in life. The mass of women, to rephrase Thoreau, lead lives of quiet gratification.

Those who have formulated identities on their own terms through crisis and commitment, through struggling for independence and self-confidence, tend to be more flexible than those who have stayed with or returned to identities rooted in childhood. But, having wrenched themselves from their roots, they also feel less certitude. Women in the Identity Achievement group make commitments, but because they have made their commitments on their own terms, they are aware that commitments can be undone and reformulated. Therefore, they have more anxiety than the Foreclosures, who view their lives as imprinted in stone, as paths that they must adapt to and follow.

Toleration of uncertainty is an aspect of experience that has not been much discussed in the psychological literature, but it appears to have profound influence on identity formation and on how one organizes one's life. Growth always involves risk. To reach for something, one must give up what one already has and take the chance that one will lose all. And one knows that there are no guarantees.

The Foreclosures are at one pole on this dimension, unable to risk or tolerate uncertainty. They organize their lives, both in adolescence and in adulthood, to be as predictable as possible. They fear the uncontrollable, and here religion tends to allay these worries. They deny that luck plays a role in their lives, too fearful of acknowledging what may be out of their control. They are women who build structure in their lives and maintain it at all costs, shunning surprise or the unexpected, making changes tentatively and as little as possible.

At the other pole are the Diffusions, so accustomed to uncertainty that they retreat to passivity, rolling with fate, taking what comes. These women feel so unable to control any aspect of their lives that they treat life as a kind of carnival ride, reacting to whatever may be around the next turn.

In the Moratoriums during their college years we most clearly see the effort to come to terms with uncertainty, and in the adult Achievements we see the balance effected. The college Moratoriums speak eloquently of their awareness of uncertainty; anything is possible. By the time they reach adulthood, they know that not everything is possible. They know that they must choose and relinquish what is not chosen. Even more, they know that their choices, their life structures, have only a degree of finality. They learn to experience certainty within a context of qualm.

While the Foreclosures experience their lives as being founded on the only reasonable choices and feel that their lives could not be unfolding otherwise, adult Achievements know that they have chosen and could just as well have chosen differently. The Achievements also know that the ground on which they stand could shake, that change can happen, change they may both welcome and dread. But because they have an internalized sense of changeableness, they feel prepared for what may come, ready to meet the next challenge. They live with more uneasiness than the Foreclosures because they know, perhaps only unconsciously but in some deep way, that nothing lasts forever and that living is change.

On Working and Loving

Too often, researchers and writers make a sharp distinction between woman as worker—productive employee or creator —and woman as relator to others, as though there were indeed two quite separate aspects of a woman that are inevitably in conflict. As Smelser (1980) points out, both work and love are dependent on interpersonal relationships and might be just different names for similar adaptive processes. The women of this study frequently stress as sources of their enjoyment in work their opportunities to care successfully for others and to interact with colleagues and the public. These interactions, in addition to their mastery of more technical skills, lead to a sense of competence (see also Baruch, Barnett, and Rivers, 1983; Fiske, 1980). Women, then, do not leave their "relating" selves behind when they go to work. Instead, as Gilligan (1982) points out, they tend to bring with them qualities of concern and care, the cornerstones of relatedness, and integrate these aspects into their aspirations for their jobs.

If women bring relatedness to the workplace, they also bring working to relationships. Contrary to a stereotypic depiction that has become part of the fabric of our assumptions, relationships are not passive endeavors. Being someone's wife or mother is not simply an ascribed pursuit, as it may have been in other times. Mature caring and its vicissitudes are complex and poorly understood (White, 1985). To care is active; it is an expression of effort. Getting along with another requires thought, initiative, and endeavor. Much of the conversation that women engage in tends to explore and analyze this realm. To discuss what others are doing, how they are handling problems, to share opinions about how difficulties might be dealt with, how feelings might be managed, how confrontations might be handled tactfully are as much aspects of work as men discussing business. They are as much an effort at mastery. Women bring creativity, ingenuity, and ideals to their relationships, whether at home or in the workplace. Skill and success in relatedness therefore become keystones of identity. A woman does not make a clear separation between relating and work.

It is difficult theoretically to describe the importance or role of working in women's lives. In studies of men (Vaillant, 1977; Levinson and others, 1978), the vicissitudes of career dominate the psychological world. Relationships are clearly present, but sound a subtheme of harmony, perhaps a steady counterpoint, clearly in the background. For women, the opposite is true. As they recount their history, group their lives into "chapters" or stages, their relational history provides the central thread and lines of demarcation. Their careers are there but largely in the background, at least through their early thirties.

For feminists and those committed to equality of opportunity for women, this finding may be troubling and embarrassing and one many would just as soon overlook. Women are not like men, and, to some, difference implies inequality. Swidler (1980), in an essay entitled "Love and Adulthood in American Culture," makes the point that American culture has never been able to make heroic the achievement of adult fidelity, commitment, intimacy, and care. Our developmental psychology, as well as our culture, has tended to equate maturity with independence and impenetrable personal boundaries, thus relegating the interpenetration of selves in relatedness to a less mature form of existence (Gutmann, 1964; Notman and others, 1986).

Whether women work, whether women have important, high-status, powerful, and prestigious positions is a different question from what role work may play in how a woman positions her sense of self in the world. Women's embeddedness in relatedness does not detract from their capacities to work, nor does noticing this embeddedness imply that women ought to be deprived of occupational equality.

The finding that relatedness rather than career ambition is central to identity in women correlates with clinical data from those who treat women. I have worked with many highly successful professional women who spend two years in intensive psychotherapy and scarcely mention their work. Their emotional energy and their sense of conflict are invested in their relationships, usually with men, in their effort to find a personal and emotional source of validation. Work success does not compensate for unfulfilled needs for human relatedness.

That work is not the central anchor of women's identity explains to some extent how easily and quickly shifts in female employment took place. Women's liberation was a fast revolution. Between 1968 (when these women entered college) and 1980, the percentage of women in the work force rose from 42 percent to 52 percent (U.S. Department of Labor, 1985). Among the women in this study, work identities were assumed unambivalently and easily in the sense that few women spoke of much internal conflict about whether to work. They simply assumed that they would, despite the fact that few of them had mothers who worked. For most, economic factors were a concern, but, more, the prevailing social climate had shifted in favor of employment for women. It was not necessary to become a feminist to be employed or to have a career. Nor was it necessary for women who were employed to internally rework important identifications with their mothers. Work life was simply grafted on, an additional pursuit with varying degrees of importance to different women but not a psychologically wrenching transformation.

We leave these women here at midlife. For the past ten years, the biological clock has been a dominant pacer of life as they have had to come to terms, one way or the other, with their potential for motherhood. Having decided that question, they will find situational variables exerting some control on future decisions (Stewart, 1980). Yet, there will be additional choices and time left for realization of nascent goals, goals that have been kept on the back burner, and goals not yet contemplated. Choices made will stencil, but not determine, the choices yet to come.

Theoretical and Research Implications

The longitudinal data of this study show that the separation-individuation phase of adolescence is critical to identity formation in adulthood. Although women individuate less than men, they vary in how much they seek to become individuated selves. A continuum of separation-individuation underlies the four identity status categories; in fact, these categories themselves may be no more than an artificial way of slicing that continuum. At one end lie the Foreclosures, those who have not separated or individuated very much. If one remains a Foreclosure by the end of college, one's future life is quite predictable unless untoward events block the chosen path and force reconsideration. At the other end are the Diffusions, who have separated and individuated too much, too early. They did not internalize enough identity-forming structure from their parents to be able to crystallize a workable identity. Moratoriums, who would be placed nearer the Diffusions on this continuum, have a strongly internalized sense of who they are supposed to be, but they try to break away from this self too drastically, too painfully. Some are able to bear the pain and move on to Achieved identities. Others become overwhelmed and return to essentially Foreclosed positions. The Identity Achievements, in between the Foreclosures and Moratoriums, tend to separate from their childhood selves gradually and incrementally, preserving relatedness at each step. Their growth is best described as a process of ongoing rapprochement: moving forward, touching base, moving forward in a rhythm that continues into adulthood.

What, then, determines which form of identity resolution a young woman will experience? Ultimately, identity formation is a process unique to each individual. Nevertheless, enough similarities exist within each group to warrant an attempt at generalization. Much of the difference among the groups, when they are viewed as college seniors, rests in their history of obtaining good feelings about themselves. The history of both positive/rewarding and negative/punishing transactions with others becomes internalized and later structuralized as the superego. The child, until adolescence, has an inner agent of the parents determining when she is good and when she is bad. The developmental problem of adolescence is to shift the inner psychological balance so that the superego has less power and the ego—the reality principle—has more. This process is concomitant to the process of separation-individuation because the superego is the main repository of childhood expectations and identifications. It harbors both the internalized policeman and the caring, loving emissary of the parents.

Foreclosures as young girls had harmonious, gratifying relationships with their families. They were "good girls," doing what was right. For them, the adolescent task jeopardizes a too-harmonious inner balance, and so they seek to avoid the psychological tasks of adolescence by re-creating an environment where the old balance can continue to be effective. They experience no push to individuate and may harshly judge others who do.

The Identity Achievements start with a similar ego-superego configuration, but the superego never had as much of a monopoly on self-esteem. Although no more talented than the Foreclosures, they tend to value competence more for its own sake than for its role in pleasing others. They also have more capacity to tolerate anxiety and guilt, which occur when they do not please others or meet their own inner standards. They experience more stress and pain than the Foreclosures but gain in flexibility.

The Moratoriums attempt to battle their superego head on, denying at times that it exists at all. But they cannot quite bring themselves to give up the experience of being good. As a result, they tend, during late adolescence, to swing back and forth, trying to hold on to the loving functions of the superego with one hand and to abolish it with the other. The extremes of identity confusion among the Moratoriums during college are the outward sign of the intensity of the internal separation-individuation struggle, despite their conscious denials and externalizations of it. And, as the follow-up data show, the struggle can have varying outcomes, depending partly on external circumstance.

The Diffusions, as we have seen, are confronting, during college, a struggle of a different kind. Lacking the building blocks that the other statuses are trying to rearrange, they are questing for parts of the self that they failed to develop at earlier times of their lives.

Do these data tell us anything about how to produce someone in one or the other of these statuses? The answer must be very guarded. Clearly whatever helps the growing girl develop a sense of competence in her own abilities, independent of the praise of others, will be helpful to her in achieving an identity. Whatever helps her identify and value her inner experiences, her wishes, tastes, reactions, her very selfhood will serve her well in formulating who she uniquely will come to be. And someone must be there with her, supporting and validating her, rather than directing or holding her too close. The process of separation-individuation, crucial to identity formation, is yet little understood and so much an internal one that it is difficult to determine how external conditions either foster or inhibit its unfolding. In separation-individuation lies the balance between self and other in ongoing relatedness as well as the degree of freedom a woman allows herself to explore the boundaries of what she might become.

And if we did know how to produce a woman in one or the other of these statuses, would we want to? Clearly, Identity

Diffusion is an undesirable state, and it is important to learn to identify it early and to intervene therapeutically to remedy it. The other statuses, however, represent differences in style, in values, in ways of searching for meaning in life. The Foreclosures are rigid, but they are solid, dependable, and content. The Identity Achievements are more anxious, more discontent, but they are also more creative and more adventurous. Those who were Moratoriums in college, as we have seen, have largely resolved the crisis in one direction or another but maintain their greater tendency to psychological awareness and self-reflectiveness and also their greater existential angst and dissatisfaction. These identity statuses, then, describe different pathways through the identity formation maze. The ultimate success of one or another resolution may not be clear until much later in adulthood.*

To study separation-individuation in women is a disorienting task because women tend to grow within rather than out of relationships. Often the phenomena of a woman's life represent both separation and interrelatedness at the same time. We have seen, for example, how adolescent women sometimes unfetter themselves from their mothers' influence by subordinating themselves to their boyfriends' influence. Is this separation and individuation? The answer can only be that it is separation-individuation of a particularly female kind.

The developmental history of separation-individuation is different for women and men. What Levinson (Levinson and others, 1978) calls "the Dream" for men—a man's vision of his future self, cast in occupational or agentic terms—does not exist in the same way among these women. For women, "the Dream" is painted in relational terms, who they will be for others and who will be in their network. Women's development is based on an ongoing balance between self-in-world and self-in-relation. A developmental psychology of women must describe autonomy

---

*The contrasts in style between the Foreclosures and the Achievements and Moratoriums parallel findings by Lowenthal and others (1975) that people with simple rather than complex psychological structures were happiest in their lives, especially in later life.

and connectedness and the arc between them. The problem again is the lack of language. We do not have words to annotate the discourse of intimacy and mutuality: It is so much easier to describe in words what someone is doing than how they value others or connect others to the self. Nor can we adequately chronicle the nuances of our relationships with those people whom we keep inside ourselves to help us define ourselves even when we are alone.

Psychological theory that bases itself on the importance of a woman's separation from her mother is misguided and in error. A theory of the separation-individuation process that underlies identity formation in women must appreciate that women never fully separate from their mothers. This relationship is crucially important to women at least through their early adulthood. Mothers continue to play not only an important internal role in the lives of these women but an external one as well (see also Fischer, 1986; Cohler and Grunebaum, 1981). A woman's identity is always poised in contradistinction to and in the context of her mother's.

We must, however, take into account here that few of these women had professional mothers or even mothers who worked when these women were children. Therefore, competition with mother is cast only in relational terms. The fate of female ambition may change once women have a same-sexed parental model in the world of work to measure themselves against.

In this work world, most women do not have mentors. This sociological observation is important to anyone concerned about harnessing female talent to the public sphere of work. The most ambitious women in this sample, the ones who are most clearly striving to achieve in the larger world, are those with graduate training and who gained a mentor through this experience. For the other women, even those who are professionals, such as elementary schoolteachers, nurses, and physical therapists, work has meaning because of the personal rewards of helping others or because of the association with colleagues. Work is thus translated into relational terms and enjoyed on that basis. For these women, self-esteem is based primarily on how they are doing in the family; work identity is tangential.

Hopes and dreams are in the family; work does not claim their spirit. Perhaps we as a society need to wonder why there are so few mentors for women.

Women make life choices, which may include occupational goals, on the basis of what will bring them emotional gratification, again stressing relational terms. Contentment and happiness remain more important than ambition. We, as yet, have no good means to measure these trite-sounding elements, which are nevertheless women's central organizing forces. Religion, a highly significant aspect of many women's lives, has also not been given enough attention in any psychological theory. Politics tends not to be a defining arena of identity unless an issue directly touches their lives. Ideology in women is fundamentally interpersonal.

In short, the aspects most salient to identity formation in women have been overlooked by psychological research and theory, which stresses the growth of independence and autonomy as hallmarks of adulthood. Communion, connection, relational embeddedness, spirituality, affiliation—with these women construct an identity. This is not to suggest that women cannot succeed, achieve, wield power, or govern nations as well as men. They can and do. Rather, it is to emphasize that such activities will have a place in an identity that is uniquely female in form.

Appendix A

Investigating
Women's Identity:
Methods and Samples

The aim of sampling was to obtain a cross-sectional, representative sample of college women in their senior year. The reason for choosing college seniors was the theoretically derived prediction that identity status would be more stable at this point than earlier, the women having had the benefit of three years of college in which to consider alternatives and being faced with making important decisions for their future.

Samples

Sample I. In 1971, names of senior women were drawn, at random, from class lists of three institutions: a large, coeducational, private university; a large, coeducational, state university; and a small, private, somewhat exclusive women's college. Forty-eight women were included in order to have twelve women in each of the four identity statuses. Interviewing continued until the criterion of twelve subjects in each category was met.

In that universities and colleges often have identifiable characters and, as a result, draw certain kinds of students, three were included in order to minimize any purely local and specific effects. Those women attending the state university were, for example, likely to be living at home, while those attending the women's college generally lived on campus. Students at the large, private university most often held part-time jobs and paid all or part of their own tuition. As a result of the diversity of institutions, all these life-styles were represented in the sample.

Sample II. Twelve additional women were interviewed in 1973. These women were randomly drawn from another large, state university in a different part of the country. They were to be part of another study that was never completed.

Sample III: The Follow-Up Study. In 1983, an effort was made to locate each of the sixty women for whom data were available. Because many had changed their names through marriage or moved or both, only forty could be found. Current addresses were obtained through alumnae lists, where possible, or through family members if they remained at the former address of the subject. Telephone directories in the subjects' cities of origin were consulted to try to find people with the same last names who might lead us to the subjects. (Women who had common last names, such as Smith, were least likely to be found.) Of the forty located in this manner, two were deceased; an interview with a family member supplied information about one of these women. Five women refused to participate in the follow-up study. Therefore, thirty-four subjects constitute this sample. In original identity-status groupings, there are eight women each in the Foreclosure, Achievement, and Diffusion groups, and ten Moratoriums.

There was no apparent systematic bias in the group of women who participated in the follow-up. As this is meant to be a descriptive study, the sample seems to be a good enough representation of a reasonable cross-section of women.

The women in the follow-up study were reinterviewed between 1983 and 1985.

Method

First Data Collection. Subjects were contacted by letter, which described the study as an investigation of the psychology of women. Several days later, they were phoned and invited to participate; 75 percent of the women accepted. Interviews were conducted at the subject's convenience, and a small stipend was offered.

Each subject was interviewed with Marcia's Identity-Status Interview (see Appendix B), a procedure that takes from a half hour to one hour. Interviews were tape recorded and later rated by an advanced female clinical psychology graduate student. Thirty of the interviews were rated by a second rater, also a female clinical psychology graduate student, in order to establish reliability. There was agreement on twenty-seven of the overall status ratings, a 90 percent reliability. The remaining three tapes were rated by a third rater, and the subjects were assigned to the statuses that received two ratings. If a two-out-of-three criterion (which has been used in some of Marcia's work) were used, the reliability in this study would rise to 100 percent. On four tapes that were not rated as part of the reliability assessment, the rater indicated some question about the category assignment of a subject; those tapes also received a second rating.

Following the Identity-Status Interview, subjects were interviewed for one-and-a-half to two hours using an open-ended semistructured interview protocol (see Appendix B). The purpose of this interview was to elicit revealing and salient developmental processes by encouraging the subject to speak associatively and introspectively about her life. The interview format, a series of possible topics, was intended as a guide for the interviewer, but the interviews were clinical in nature, unstructured but, we hoped, deepening, following affect where it might go.

Each tape was later evaluated by me and one other clinical psychologist, who took notes and commented on the tapes. We focused our notes on biographical information, central conflicts and their management, object relationships, defensive structures, identification processes, descriptions of family members, important psychosocial forces, affect and fantasy material. Dreams and early memories were recorded verbatim.

The procedure for Sample II was essentially the same except that the interview was lengthened to include more early memories and each subject was also given a set of Thematic Apperception Test cards to respond to.

Second Data Collection. By 1983, these women were all over the country, and data collection required some ingenuity. Subjects were contacted by letter, reminded of their earlier participation in this study, and advised that they would be sent a questionnaire. The questionnaire was sent along with a blank cassette tape for those who preferred recording answers to writing them. These materials were followed by phone calls. Assembling the data took approximately two years. Some women agreed to be interviewed in person but never found the time to complete the questionnaire. In these instances, personal interviews followed the questionnaires. Some women returned sketchy questionnaires but were amenable to personal or telephone interviews to broaden the material. Other women returned several hours of tape-recorded answers to the questions. Because of the demands on people's time to complete such a broad and deep questionnaire, the method of data collection for each subject was devised to suit her needs. Personal interviews averaged three to four hours. Subjects reported that it took three to four hours to complete the questionnaire in written form. Telephone interviews to resolve what I did not understand in written questionnaires averaged one to two hours.

The intent of the second data collection was to review as thoroughly as possible the parameters and choices of a woman's life since she left college. Subjects were asked to respond again to the questions of the Identity-Status Interview. Identity status was not formally rated for the follow-up data because there is no validation for using the standard Identity-Status Interview with an older sample. The criteria used for rating the categories have less meaning as one is chronologically farther from adolescence. Instead of devising a formal rating procedure, I chose to give my impressions of current identity constellations and to document my conclusions with the case material.

Besides the identity-status questions, the questionnaire/interview protocol (see Appendix B) covered work history, work satisfactions and dissatisfactions, relationship history, moments of crucial decision making as well as open-ended questions that invited the subjects to reflect on their lives.

Although my students were helpful as research assistants

and did two of the interviews, I did most of the interviewing and stayed close to the data and the actual women who provided it. Rather than follow a rigid format for collecting the follow-up data, I attempted to get to know each subject as thoroughly as possible with the means available.

Data Analysis and Case Presentation

In that each woman has unique pieces to fit together to form her identity, cases were analyzed individually, and the portrait drawn included all salient material presented by that woman. Both the nature and depth of material varied from woman to woman. Some women gave only general characterizations of their early life; others provided sharp detail. Memory varied: Some had rich, complex memories; others remembered little of their childhoods. Women also varied in the number of experiences they had as adults. Some had distinct and separate periods of adulthood; others had lives that were more continuous. When individual cases are presented in this book, I have omitted unrevealing responses to questions, but I have tried to include the themes and events that seemed to be important for each woman. Because each woman is unique, each case presentation is somewhat different.

After the individual portraits were completed, I looked across the women in each group to try to understand common themes. Where advisable, statistical analyses were performed. The general comments I make about each group derive from this set of analyses.

Appendix B

Interviews Used
in the Study

Identity-Status Interview

Introduction

- Where are you from? Where are you living now?
- How did you happen to come to this college?
- Did your father go to college? Where? What does he do now?
- Did your mother go to college? Where? What does she do now?

Occupation

- What are you majoring in? What do you plan to do with it?
- When did you come to decide on _____? Did you ever consider anything else?
- What seems attractive about _____?
- Most parents have plans for their children, things they would like them to go into or do. Did yours have any plans like that for you?
- How do your parents feel about your plans now?
- How willing do you think you'd be to change if something better came along? (What might be better in your terms?)
- Do you plan to marry? Do you plan to work after you marry? Why or why not?
- Do you plan to have children? Work after you have children? Why or why not?

Source: Adapted from Marcia (1964) and Schenkel and Marcia (1972).

198

- Do you expect to take time off from work when you have children?
- How do you plan to combine work and marriage and child-rearing? What problems do you think might exist? How do you feel these might be solved? Have you ever felt differently about this? How does the man in your life feel about these things? How important would it be to you that he agree about these things?

Religion

- Do you have any particular religious affiliation or preference?
- How about your folks?
- Ever very active in church? How about now? Do you get into many religious discussions?
- How do your parents feel about your beliefs now?
- Are yours any different from theirs?
- Was there any time when you came to doubt any of your religious beliefs? When?
- How did it happen? How did you resolve your questions? How are things for you now?

Politics

- Do you have any particular political preference?
- How about your parents?
- Ever take any kind of political action—join groups, write letters, participate in demonstrations, etc.?
- Any issues you feel pretty strongly about?
- Any particular time when you decided on your political beliefs?

Sex

- What are your views on premarital intercourse? What criteria do you use to determine your actions?
- Have you always felt this way? Have you ever had any doubts? How did you resolve them?

- What would your parents think about your sexual standards and behavior?
- Do you feel there is ever any conflict between your ideas, emotions, and behavior?
- Could you give an example? How do you handle the conflicts? How frequently do they occur?

Clinical Identity Interview

1. If there's a person who you want to know you, what sorts of things would you tell them about yourself?
2. What was most important in the last two or three years in terms of making you the way you are? What influenced you most? Before that—say, during high school? How about before that—like in elementary school?
3. In the last few years, who of all the people that you've known during that time did you like most? Before that? (You've talked about boyfriends and pals. Is there someone that you liked in a different way?)
4. Who of all these people did you most want to be like? Did you become like them in any way? Who of all the people that you know now would you most like to be like?
5. Right now, what is the thing you like to do most? If you had a lot of free time, what would you put it to? (Is that what you'd put your life to?) (In a more general sense, what would you like to put your life to if you could arrange things any way you'd like?) (What would you do? Is it something you've seriously thought to putting your life to?) Now, how far would you go to do that? How much trouble would you really take for this? Would you delay status, marriage, money, take real risks?
6. How do you imagine your future in the next year? In the next five years? In ten years?
7. All of us have daydreams, even though we don't necessarily take them seriously. What kinds of things do you daydream about? Is there a daydream that you've had continuously, something you like to daydream about when you listen to music or are alone?

8. What is the last night dream you remember?
9. Just on the spur of the moment, what is the earliest thing you can remember? (When was that?) Another one?

Addition for Sample II

Earliest memory of your mother? Father? Earliest memory in which you were very happy? Earliest in which you were very unhappy?

Longitudinal Study Follow-Up Questionnaire and Interview Format

Part I: Identity

The following are similar to questions asked of you in the original study. We are interested in understanding how your views or choices have or have not changed over the past ten years.

A. *Occupation*

-   Did you pursue the occupation that you had chosen in college? If yes, has it fulfilled your expectations? Please describe. If not, why not? How did you come to choose another?
-   If your occupational goals or expectations have changed since 1971, how have they changed?
-   How likely do you think it is that you will remain in your current occupation? What alternatives are you considering?

B. *Religion*

-   What religion do you practice?
-   How committed to your religion are you? What does your religious commitment involve?
-   Have your religious views or practices changed in the past ten years? If so, what brought about these changes?

C. *Politics*

- How involved in political issues are you? Which political issues do you feel most strongly about?
- Did you vote in the last Presidential election?
- Are you active in local, community, or national politics? What do/did you do?
- Have your political views or preferences changed over the past ten years? If so, how?

D. *Sex*

- How have your views about sexual morality—premarital, marital, or extramarital sex—changed over the past ten years?
- What statement would you make to define your own *principles* in regard to your own sexual behavior?
- What principles might you want your daughter to follow in regard to sexual morality? (Please answer this question even if you don't have a daughter.)

Part II: Educational and Occupational History

A. *Education*

Please describe your education past high school:

Institution   Program (course of study)   Degree   Dates
1.
2.
3.

Do you plan to pursue further education? Please describe your plans.

B. *Work History*

- Have you worked outside the home since graduation from college?

- Please give occupational titles and dates:

| *Position* | *Duties* | *Dates* |
| (Title) | (What you do/did) | |

- How did you choose your first job? If outside the field of your college major, please explain how you came to decide on this occupational choice.
- Please explain your reasons for any subsequent job changes. Why did you leave one job for the next?
- If there has been a period over the last ten years when you have not held a job, please explain.
- For periods when you have not held a job, please describe your pursuits.
- Describe your current employment: What do you do? In what ways is it satisfactory to you? In what ways unsatisfactory? What is the most important gratification you derive from your job? Which aspects of your job do you find to be most difficult?
- Have there been people (or one specific person) who have strongly influenced your career direction or goals? If so, please describe them and how they influenced or guided you.
- From an occupational viewpoint, what direction do you see your life taking in the future? What do you hope to be doing ten years from now?

Part III: Personal History

A. *Family*

_____ Single, never married. Please begin with question 1.
_____ Married. Please begin with question 7.
_____ Separated or divorced. Please begin with question 1.

_____ Remarried. Please begin with question 7. Do questions 7-12 for second marriage, 13-15 for first marriage, and all remaining questions.

1. Do you plan to remain single? Please explain.
2. Describe your current dating patterns. How important has dating been to you?
3. Are you currently involved in a love relationship? Please describe its role in your life.
4. If you are engaged or living with someone, do you plan to marry this person? Please explain your situation with regard to the decisions involved.

If you are separated or divorced, go to question 7.
If you are single and never married, please continue.

5. Please describe any other love relationships that have been significant in your life over the past ten years. How long have they lasted? What brought them to an end?
6. What do you want most in a love relationship?

Please go to question 16.

7. When did you marry? Please describe the circumstances under which you married: How did you meet? How long did you know each other before marriage? What kind of wedding did you have? What led you to decide to marry this particular man?

If you are separated or divorced, go to question 13.
If you are married or remarried, please continue.

8. What is your husband's age, occupation, and educational background?
9. How do you fit together as a couple? How do you complement each other? In what ways do you clash?
10. How has your marriage changed you?
11. How has your marriage fulfilled your needs? How has it not fulfilled your wishes? How would you like it to be different?

12. Have you had any serious marital problems? Have you seriously considered separation? If so, please describe the areas of difficulty.
13. If you have been separated or divorced since 1971, please discuss the decision to end the marriage.

    If you have not separated or divorced since 1971, go to question 16.

14. How did your marriage change you?
15. How did the separation or divorce change you or your life? Please describe your experiences after the separation or divorce.
16. Do you have children? *If not, go to question 22.*

    Name   *Sex*   *Age*

    Are there particular ages of your children's development that you have found particularly enjoyable or frustrating? Why?

17. Please discuss how you came to decide to have your first child at that particular time in your life. How did you decide on timing of subsequent children?
18. Do you plan to have more children? If so, when and under what circumstances? If not, why not?
19. How has having children changed the person that you are? What aspects of your life (self, love relationship, career) have been enriched by motherhood, and what aspects have been diminished?
20. How are your views about raising children the same or different from the way your parents raised you?
21. What has been the most difficult aspect about being a mother? What have you found hardest to adjust to? How would you like things to be different?

    Go to question 23.

22. If you do not have children now, do you plan to have them? Why or why not? Please explain.

23.   Have you had any miscarriages, abortions, or still-
        births? What effect has this event(s) had on you?

B.   *General Circumstances*

1.   What has your financial situation been like in the past
        ten years? Have you had to struggle financially, or
        have you been financially secure?
2.   Describe your health over the past ten years.
        Describe your use of alcohol, tobacco, and drugs.
3.   In what type of setting, city or country, have you
        lived during the past ten years?
4.   How many times have you moved in the past ten years?
5.   Have you ever been in psychotherapy or counseling?
        If so, when?

If any of these factors in Part B have been especially significant in your life, please explain.

Part IV: Personal Growth

1.   What is the very earliest thing you can remember in your
        life? Please describe in detail the very first memory you
        have of some specific event.
2.   What is the second earliest thing you can remember in
        your life?
3.   Try to see your life as a series of chapters, beginning as far
        back as you can remember. These "chapters" should group
        years that seem to belong together. What would be the
        main theme of each chapter in terms of the things that
        mattered most to you, that you most wished for or were
        trying to accomplish? What were the most important
        things that happened in each chapter?
4.   What have been the major good experiences in your life in
        the past ten years?
5.   What have been the major bad experiences in your life in
        the past ten years?
6.   What have been the major turning points in your life in

the past ten years? What have been the critical decisions you have made?

7. In what way has luck—or fortune—played an important role in your life? How much do you feel that you have been the architect of your own destiny?

8. Looking back, who have been the most important people in your life? Why?

List in order the ten people to whom you feel closest:

Name	Relationship to You	How Long Known
1.		
2.		
3.		
4.		
5.		
6.		
7.		
8.		
9.		
10.		

Please put a star next to those people to whom you feel *very* close. Please put a circle next to those people to whom you would turn for help in a crisis.

9. How would you describe your college years? How have the experiences you had in college most affected your life?

10. If you had it to do over again, what would you change about your college years?

11. Describe your current relationships with your parents and siblings. How have these relationships changed over the past ten years?

12. As you look back, how are you the product of your family? How are you different from them?

13. How many of your friends from college do you still feel close to?

14. How important have friendships been in your life? How has the experience of friendship changed over the years?

15. What are your major hobbies or interests and how important have they been for you?

16. What has been your philosophy over rough spots? How have you coped with stress?

17. What are your hopes, dreams, and plans for the future? How do you want your life to change in the future? In what ways do you hope to become different as a person in the future?

18. What do you most fear in the future?

19. Imagine yourself at age eighty looking over your life. What would you be most satisfied to have accomplished or experienced in your life? What are the accomplishments in your life so far of which you feel most proud?

20. If there is anything else of unique significance in your life in terms of influences, experiences, or relationships, please describe them here.

References

Adelson, J., and Doehrman, M. "The Psychodynamic Approach to Adolescence." In J. Adelson (Ed.), *Handbook of Adolescent Psychology.* New York: Wiley, 1980.

Aries, E., and Olver, R. "Sex Differences in the Development of a Separate Sense of Self During Infancy: Directions for Future Research." *Psychology of Women Quarterly,* 1985, *9,* 515-532.

Bakan, D. *The Duality of Human Existence.* Boston: Beacon Press, 1966.

Balser, B. H. (Ed.). *Psychotherapy of the Adolescent.* New York: International Universities Press, 1957.

Baruch, G., Barnett, R., and Rivers, C. *Lifeprints.* New York: Signet, 1983.

Belenky, M., and others. *Women's Ways of Knowing.* New York: Basic Books, 1986.

Bernard, J. *Sex Differences: An Overview.* Module 26. New York: MSS Modular Publications, 1974.

Bilsker, D., Schiedel, D., and Marcia, J. E. "Sex Differences in Identity Formation." Unpublished manuscript, 1987.

Blos, P. *On Adolescence.* New York: Free Press, 1962.

Blos, P. "The Second Individuation Process of Adolescence." *Psychoanalytic Study of the Child,* 1967, *22,* 162-186.

Bourne, E. "The State of Research on Ego Identity: A Review and Appraisal. Part I." *Journal of Youth and Adolescence,* 1978a, *7,* 223-252.

Bourne, E. "The State of Research on Ego Identity: A Review

and Appraisal. Part II." *Journal of Youth and Adolescence,* 1978b, *7,* 371–392.

Chodorow, N. *The Reproduction of Mothering.* Berkeley: University of California Press, 1978.

Cohler, B., and Grunebaum, H. *Mothers, Grandmothers, and Daughters.* New York: Wiley, 1981.

Coleman, J. *The Adolescent Society.* New York: Free Press, 1961.

Douvan, E., and Adelson, J. *The Adolescent Experience.* New York: Wiley, 1966.

Eichenbaum, L., and Orbach, S. *Understanding Women.* New York: Basic Books, 1983.

Erikson, E. H. *Childhood and Society.* New York: Norton, 1950.

Erikson, E. H. "The Problem of Ego Identity." *Journal of the American Psychoanalytic Association,* 1956, *4,* 56–121.

Erikson, E. H. *Young Man Luther.* New York: Norton, 1958.

Erikson, E. H. *Identity, Youth and Crisis.* New York: Norton, 1968.

Erikson, E. H. *Life History and the Historical Moment.* New York: Norton, 1975.

Fairbairn, W. R. D. *Psychoanalytic Studies of the Personality.* London: Tavistock, 1952.

Ferree, M. "Class, Housework, and Happiness: Women's Work and Life Satisfaction." *Sex Roles,* 1984, *11,* 1057–1074.

Fischer, L. R. *Linked Lives.* New York: Harper & Row, 1986.

Fiske, M. "Changing Hierarchies of Commitment in Adulthood." In N. J. Smelser and E. Erikson (Eds.), *Themes of Work and Love in Adulthood.* Cambridge, Mass.: Harvard University Press, 1980.

Fountain, G. "Adolescent into Adult: An Inquiry." *Journal of the American Psychoanalytic Association,* 1961, *9,* 417–433.

Freud, A. "Adolescence." *Psychoanalytic Study of the Child,* 1958, *16,* 225–278.

Freud, S. "Femininity." In *Standard Edition.* Vol. 22. London: Hogarth Press, 1964. (Originally published 1933.)

Fromm, E. *Escape from Freedom.* New York: Holt, 1941.

Gilligan, C. *In a Different Voice.* Cambridge, Mass.: Harvard University Press, 1979.

Ginsburg, S. D., and Orlofsky, J. L. "Ego Identity Status, Ego Development, and Locus of Control in College Women." *Journal of Youth and Adolescence,* 1981, *10* (4), 297–307.

Gutmann, D. "An Exploration of Ego Configurations in Middle and Later Life." In B. Neugarten (Ed.), *Personality in Middle and Later Life.* New York: Atherton, 1964.

Hall, D., and Gordon, F. "Career Choices of Married Women: Effects on Conflict, Role Behavior and Satisfaction." *Journal of Applied Psychology,* 1973, *58* (10), 42–48.

Hodgson, J., and Fischer, J. "Pathways of Identity Development in College Women." *Sex Roles,* 1981, *7,* 681–690.

Hopkins, L. "Assessment of Identity Status in College Women Using Outer Space and Inner Space Interviews." *Sex Roles,* 1982, *8,* 557–565.

Johnson, M., and others. "Sexual Preference, Feminism and Women's Perceptions of the Parents." *Sex Roles,* 1981, *7,* 1–18.

Josselson, R. "Psychodynamic Aspects of Identity Formation in College Women." *Journal of Youth and Adolescence,* 1973, *2,* 3–52.

Josselson, R. "Ego Development in Adolescence." In J. Adelson (Ed.), *Handbook of Adolescent Psychology.* New York: Wiley, 1980.

Josselson, R. "Personality Structure and Identity Status in Women as Viewed Through Early Memories." *Journal of Youth and Adolescence,* 1982, *11* (4), 293–299.

Josselson, R., Greenberger, E., and McConochie, D. "Phenomenological Aspects of Psychosocial Maturity in Adolescence Part II: Girls." *Journal of Youth and Adolescence,* 1977, *6,* 145–167.

Josselyn, I. M. *The Adolescent and His World.* New York: Family Service Association of America, 1952.

Josselyn, I. M. "The Ego in Adolescence." *American Journal of Orthopsychiatry,* 1954, *24,* 223–237.

Kacerguis, M. A., and Adams, G. R. "Erikson Stage Resolution:

The Relationship Between Identity and Intimacy." *Journal of Youth and Adolescence,* 1980, *9,* 117–126.

Kaplan, A. "The 'Self-in-Relation': Implications for Depression in Women." *Psychotherapy,* 1986, *23,* 234–242.

Kaplan, A., and Klein, R. "The Relational Self in Late Adolescent Women." In *Work in Progress.* Wellesley, Mass.: Stone Center for Developmental Services and Studies, 1985.

Kernberg, O. *Object Relations Theory and Clinical Psychoanalysis.* New York: Aronson, 1976.

Lerman, H. "From Freud to Feminist Personality Theory: Getting Here from There." *Psychology of Women Quarterly,* 1986, *10,* 1–18.

Levinson, D., and others. *The Seasons of a Man's Life.* New York: Knopf, 1978.

Lortie-Lussier, M., Schwab, C., and de Koninck, J. "Working Mothers Versus Homemakers: Do Dreams Reflect the Changing Roles of Women?" *Sex Roles,* 1985, *12* (9/10), 1009–1021.

Lowenthal, M. F., and others. *Four Stages of Life.* San Francisco: Jossey-Bass, 1975.

Maccoby, E. E., and Jacklin, C. N. *The Psychology of Sex Differences.* Stanford, Calif.: Stanford University Press, 1974.

Mahler, M., Pine, F., and Bergman, A. *The Psychological Birth of the Human Infant.* New York: Basic Books, 1975.

Mallory, M. "Longitudinal Analysis of Ego Identity Status." Unpublished doctoral dissertation, Department of Psychology, University of California, Davis, 1983.

Marcia, J. E. "Determination and Construct Validity of Ego Identity Status." Unpublished doctoral dissertation, Ohio State University, 1964.

Marcia, J. E. "Development and Validation of Ego Identity Status." *Journal of Personality and Social Psychology,* 1966, *3,* 551–558.

Marcia, J. E. "Identity Six Years After: A Follow-Up Study." *Journal of Youth and Adolescence,* 1976, *5,* 145–160.

Marcia, J. E. "Identity in Adolescence." In J. Adelson (Ed.), *Handbook of Adolescent Psychology.* New York: Wiley, 1980.

Marcia, J. E., and Friedman, M. "Ego Identity Status in College Women." *Journal of Personality,* 1970, *38,* 249–263.

May, R. *Sex and Fantasy.* New York: Norton, 1980.

Mellinger, J., and Erdwins, C. "Personality Correlates of Age and Life Roles in Adult Women." *Psychology of Women Quarterly*, 1985, *9*, 503–514.

Miller, J. B. *Toward a New Psychology of Women.* Boston: Beacon Press, 1976.

Miller, J. B. "The Development of Women's Sense of Self." In *Work in Progress*. Wellesley, Mass.: Stone Center for Developmental Services and Studies, 1984.

Morgan, E. "Toward a Reformulation of the Eriksonian Model of Female Identity Development." *Adolescence*, 1982, *17*, 199–211.

Moriarty, A. E., and Toussieng, P. W. *Adolescent Coping.* New York: Grune & Stratton, 1976.

Neugarten, B., and Datan, N. "Sociological Perspectives on the Life Cycle." In P. B. Baltes and K. W. Schaie (Eds.), *Life-Span Developmental Psychology: Personality and Socialization*. New York: Academic Press, 1973.

Notman, M. T., and others. "Themes in Psychoanalytic Understanding of Women: Some Reconsiderations of Autonomy and Affiliation." *Journal of the American Academy of Psychoanalysis*, 1986, *12*, 241–253.

Oberstone, A. "Psychological Adjustment and Life Style of Single Lesbians and Single Heterosexual Women." *Psychology of Women Quarterly*, 1976, *1* (2), 172–188.

Offer, D. *The Psychological World of the Teenager.* New York: Basic Books, 1969.

Offer, D., Ostrov, E., and Howard, K. I. *The Adolescent: A Psychological Self-Portrait.* New York: Basic Books, 1981.

Orlofsky, J. "Sex Role Orientation, Identity Formation, and Self-Esteem in College Men and Women." *Sex Roles*, 1977, *6*, 561–575.

Orlofsky, J. "Identity Formation, Achievement and Fear of Success in College Men and Women." *Journal of Youth and Adolescence*, 1978, *7*, 49–62.

Orlofsky, J., and Frank, M. "Personality Structure as Viewed Through Early Memories and Identity Status in College Men and Women." *Journal of Personality and Social Psychology*, 1986, *50* (3), 580–586.

Peck, T. "Women's Self-Definition in Adulthood: from a Different Model?" *Psychology of Women Quarterly,* 1986, *10,* 274-284.

Prager, K. "Identity Development and Self-Esteem in Young Women." *Journal of Genetic Psychology,* 1982, *141,* 177-182.

Rossi, A. "Life Span Theories and Women's Lives." *Signs,* 1980, *6* (1), 4-32.

Schafer, R. "Concepts of Self and Identity and the Experience of Separation-Individuation in Adolescence." *Psychoanalytic Quarterly,* 1973, *42,* 42-60.

Schenkel, S. "Relationship Among Ego Identity Status, Field-Independence, and Traditional Femininity." *Journal of Youth and Adolescence,* 1975, *4* (1), 73-82.

Schenkel, S., and Marcia, J. E. "Attitudes Toward Premarital Intercourse in Determining Ego Identity Status in College Women." *Journal of Personality,* 1972, *40,* 472-482.

Smelser, N. J. "Issues in the Study of Work and Love in Adulthood." In N. J. Smelser and E. Erikson (Eds.), *Themes of Work and Love in Adulthood.* Cambridge, Mass.: Harvard University Press, 1980.

Spiegel, L. A. "Comments on the Psychoanalytic Psychology of Adolescence." *Psychoanalytic Study of the Child,* 1958, *13,* 296-308.

Stewart, A. "Personality and Situation in the Prediction of Women's Life Patterns." *Psychology of Women Quarterly,* 1980, *5* (2), 195-206.

Stiver, I. "The Meaning of 'Dependency' in Female-Male Relationships." In *Work in Progress.* Wellesley, Mass.: Stone Center for Developmental Services and Studies, 1984.

Surrey, J. "The Self-in-Relation." In *Work in Progress.* Wellesley, Mass.: Stone Center for Developmental Services and Studies, 1984.

Swidler, A. "Love and Adulthood in American Culture." In N. J. Smelser and E. Erikson (Eds.), *Themes of Work and Love in Adulthood.* Cambridge, Mass.: Harvard University Press, 1980.

Toder, N., and Marcia, J. E. "Ego Identity Status and Response to Conformity Pressure in College Women." *Journal of Personality and Social Psychology,* 1973, *26,* 287-294.

Unger, R. "Through the Looking Glass: No Wonderland Yet! (The Reciprocal Relationship Between Methodology and Models of Reality)." *Psychology of Women Quarterly,* 1983, *8,* 9-32.

U.S. Department of Labor. *Handbook of Labor Statistics.* Bulletin 2217. Washington, D.C.: U.S. Government Printing Office, 1985.

Vaillant, G. *Adaptation to Life.* Boston: Little, Brown, 1977.

Waterman, A. S. "Identity Development from Adolescence to Adulthood: An Extension of Theory and a Review of Research." *Developmental Psychology,* 1982, *18* (3), 341-358.

Waterman, A. S., and Waterman, C. K. "A Longitudinal Study of Changes in Ego Identity Status During the Freshman Year at College." *Developmental Psychology,* 1971, *5,* 167-173.

Waterman, C. K., and Waterman, A. S. "Ego Identity Status and Decision Styles." *Journal of Youth and Adolescence,* 1974, *3,* 1-6.

White, M. S. "Ego Development in Adult Women." *Journal of Personality,* 1985, *53* (4), 561-574.

Winnicott, D. *Collected Papers: Through Pediatrics to Psychoanalysis.* New York: Basic Books, 1958.

Winnicott, D. *The Maturational Processes and the Facilitating Environment.* New York: International Universities Press, 1965.

Index

A

Achievements. *See* Identity Achievements

Adam, 80-82

Adams, G. R., 140

Adelson, J., 19, 22, 23, 63, 171

Adolescence: choices made in, 14-15; for Foreclosures, 63-64; for Identity Achievements, 95-96, 98; identity resolution in, 13-14; identity work in, 8-9; separation-individuation in, 19-21

Agency, and separation-individuation, 171

Alice: analysis of, 72-83; background on, 70; in college, 72-78; and group characteristics, 95-96, 97, 100, 102, 179-180; in thirties, 78-83

Amanda: analysis of, 90-95; background on, 70; in college, 90-92; and group characteristics, 96, 97, 99, 100, 101; in thirties, 92-95

Anchoring: and identity, 174-178; and rapprochement, 178

Andrea: analysis of, 83-90; background on, 70; in college, 83-86; and group characteristics, 95, 96-97, 99, 100, 103, 104; in thirties, 86-90

Androcentricity, of psychoanalytic theory, 6, 22-23

Anger, of Moratoriums, 122

Aries, E., 24

Aristotle, 15

Arnold, 84-85, 86, 87-88, 96

Attachment, and differentiation, 171-172

Authority, search for, by Moratoriums, 113

B

Bakan, D., 171

Balser, B. H., 63

Barnett, R., 183

Baruch, G., 183

Belenky, M., 4, 23

Ben, 130-131, 132, 136

Bergman, A., 16, 17

Bernard, J., 4, 5

Bilsker, D., 101

Blos, P., 15-16, 19, 63

Bob, 155-156

Bourne, E., 29, 31, 141

Brett, 154-155, 156

C

Change, openness to, and identity, 181-183

Child/adult identity, for Moratoriums, 111, 119

Children: and anchoring, 175-176; for Foreclosures, 50, 52, 57, 59-60; for Identity Achievements,

Copyright Acknowledgments